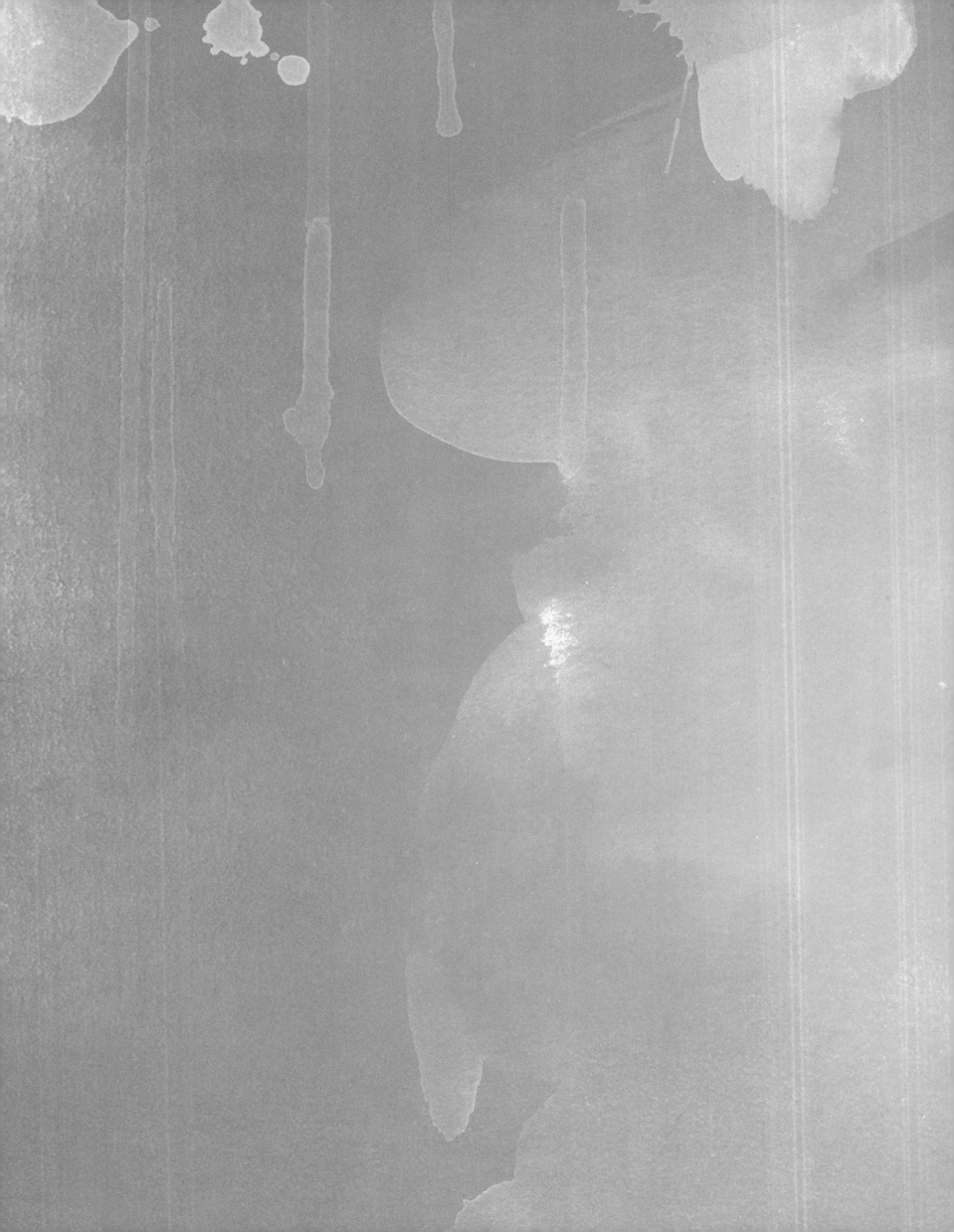

THE ATLAS OF GREAT JOURNEYS

Philip Steele

Illustrated by **Christian Gralingen**

W

WELBECK

Published in 2020 by Welbeck Children's Books
An Imprint of Welbeck Children's Limited,
part of Welbeck Publishing Group.

20 Mortimer Street, London W1T 3JW

ISBN 978 1 78312 602 6

Printed in Spain

10 9 8 7 6 5 4 3 2 1

Author: Philip Steele
Illustrator: Christian Gralingen
Supplementary Illustrator: Sam James
Digital Manager: Will Jones
Digital Consultant: Japhet Asher
Digital content: Scary Beasties Ltd
Design Manager: Emily Clarke
Editor: Joff Brown
Production: Gary Hayes

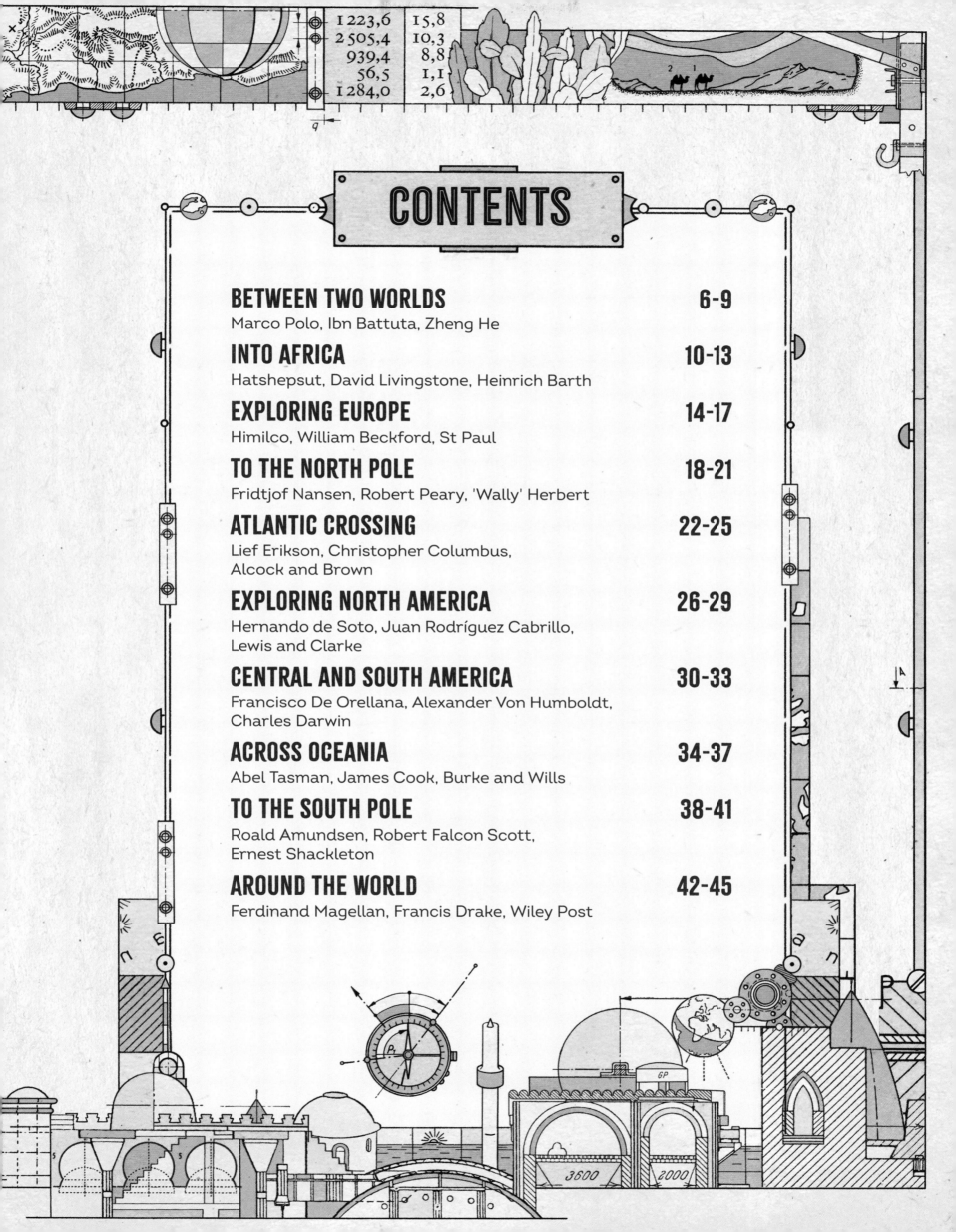

CONTENTS

INTRODUCTION

Human beings have always been explorers. Over thousands of years, we peopled the continents, crossing mountains, deserts, and eventually oceans. When Viking or Māori settlers sailed through stormy seas, they included in their numbers not just warriors, but women and children who had to be every bit as tough, inventive and brave.

In this book you will meet explorers from many different times and cultures. Some went travelling in search of trade, some in search of war, piracy or conquest. Others were refugees, fleeing war. Some journeyed for their religion, as pilgrims, missionaries, or even prisoners of repressive regimes. Some left their homes out of curiosity, always wanting to know what lay beyond the next river or mountain range. Many sought scientific knowledge, wanting to understand more about our planet.

The famous European expeditions from the 1400s to the 1700s were mostly led by men. By the 1800s, pioneering women explorers were making their mark. And in the twentieth century, female sailors, aviators and astronauts made history, gaining as much fame as ancient female leaders like the pharaoh Hatshepsut.

Today the world has shrunk. We communicate globally and travel at speed. Satellites orbit the Earth and see everything in incredible high-res detail. Sadly, they also record the damage that humans have done to the planet's oceans, rivers and forests. Today, when it's easier than ever to make our own great journeys across the globe, the history of exploration can still inspire us to new feats of endurance and adventure. It should also inspire us to care for the beautiful, unspoiled planet that filled those early explorers with such awe.

HOW TO USE THIS BOOK

The maps in this book have been enhanced with digital content that reveals the explorers' journeys in 3D.

1. Download the free **Atlas of Great Journeys** app from the Google Play Store or Apple App Store.

2. Lay the book as flat as possible in a well-lit place.

3. Launch the app and view any map page, following the on-screen instructions.

4. Touch one of the three explorer images to start the journey. An icon will move across the map, following the journey. At important points, text will pop up on the screen to explain major events and locations.

5. At each stage of the journey, you can tap on the explorer's 3D mode of transport to enlarge it, and swipe to rotate it.

MARCO POLO

Born in Venice in 1254 CE, Marco Polo traveled on the ancient Silk Road as far as China. He stayed at the court of Kublai Khan, ruler of China, for three years. The book he wrote on his return made him famous.

MARCO POLO
Venice, 1271

IBN BATTUTA
Tangier, 1325

IBN BATTUTA

Ibn Battuta was a Muslim from North Africa. In 1325 he left his hometown to go on pilgrimage to Mecca, but eventually he went on as far as India, southern Europe, East Africa, Asia, Arabia, and even China.

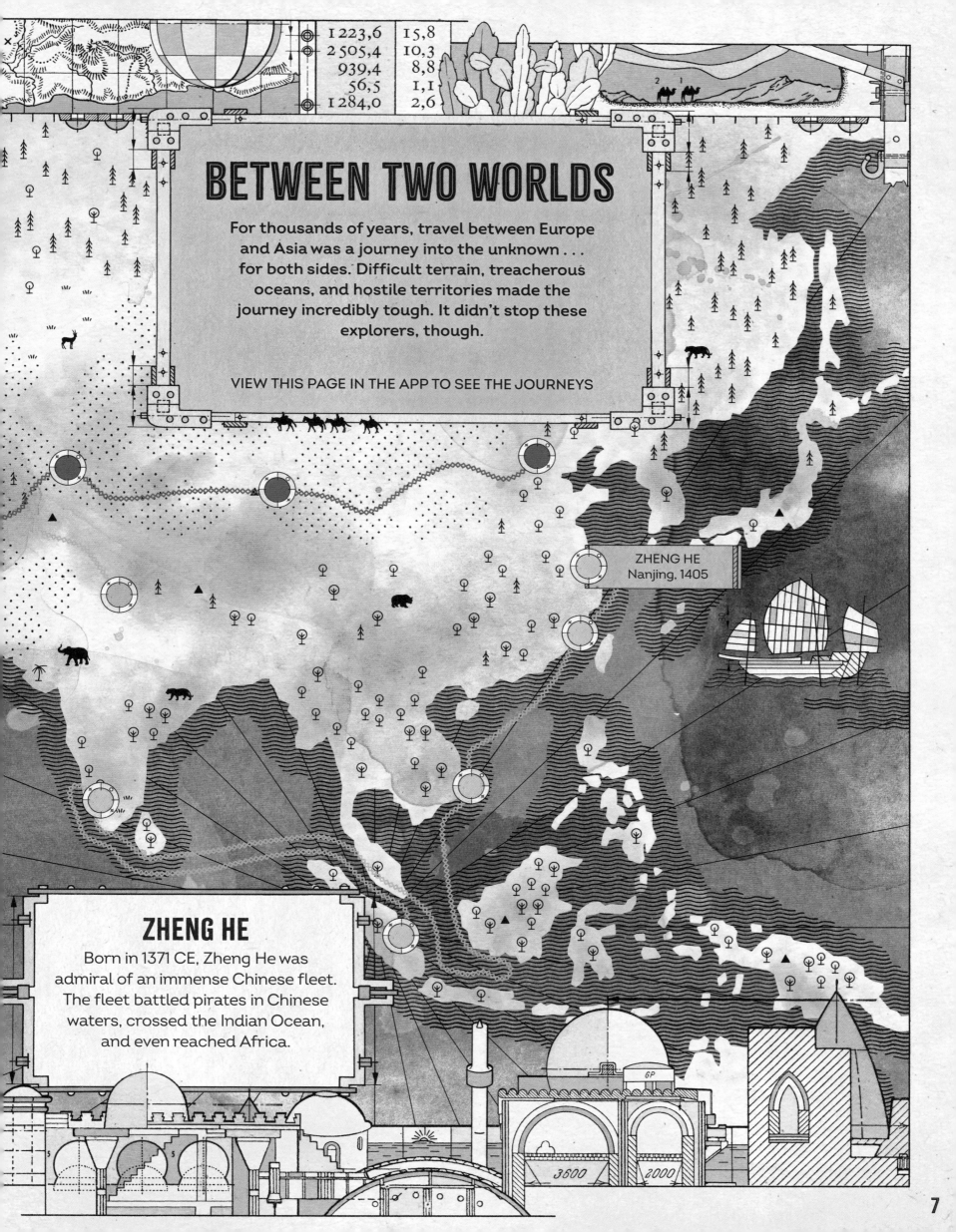

BETWEEN TWO WORLDS

For thousands of years, travel between Europe and Asia was a journey into the unknown . . . for both sides. Difficult terrain, treacherous oceans, and hostile territories made the journey incredibly tough. It didn't stop these explorers, though.

VIEW THIS PAGE IN THE APP TO SEE THE JOURNEYS

ZHENG HE
Nanjing, 1405

ZHENG HE

Born in 1371 CE, Zheng He was admiral of an immense Chinese fleet. The fleet battled pirates in Chinese waters, crossed the Indian Ocean, and even reached Africa.

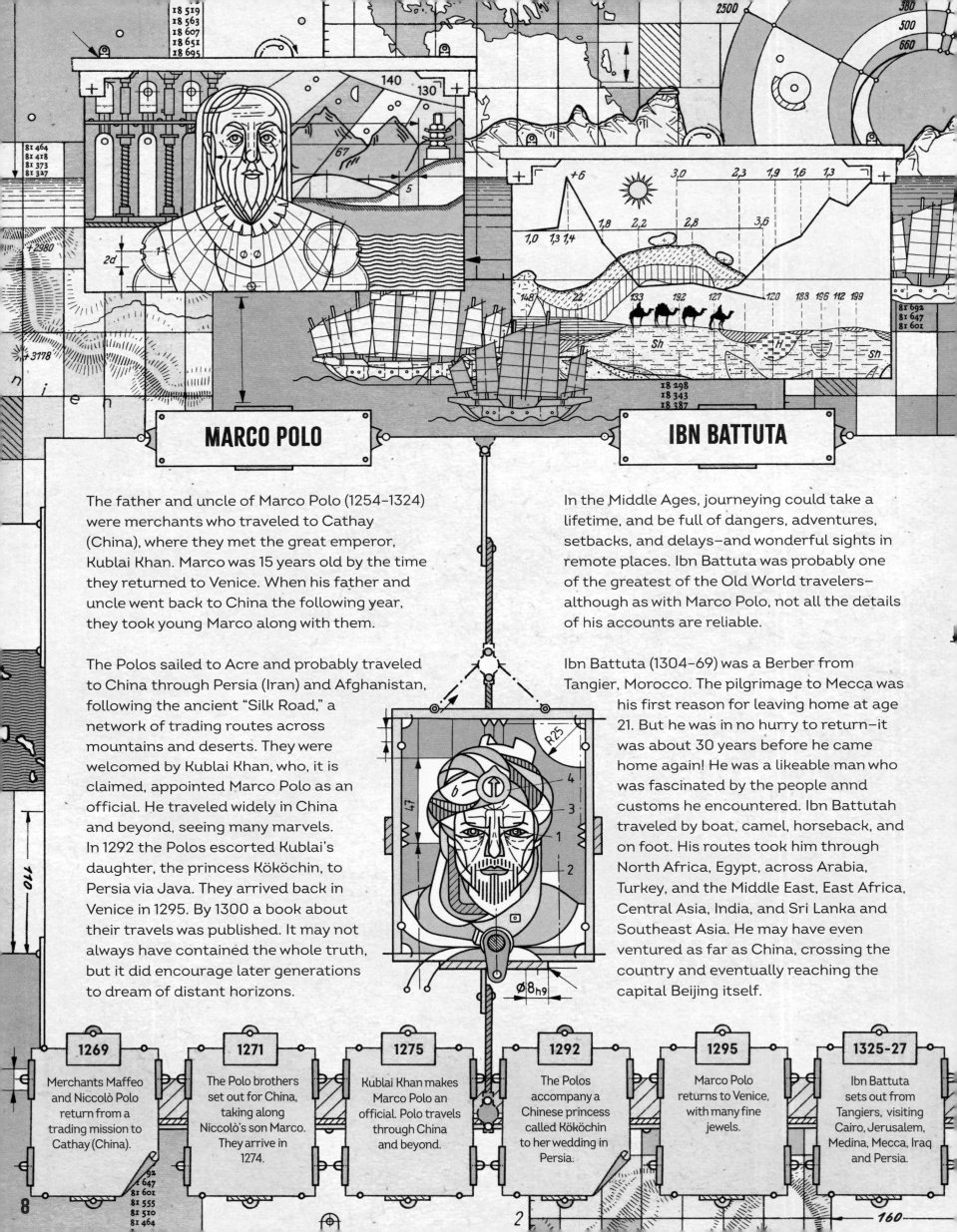

MARCO POLO

IBN BATTUTA

The father and uncle of Marco Polo (1254–1324) were merchants who traveled to Cathay (China), where they met the great emperor, Kublai Khan. Marco was 15 years old by the time they returned to Venice. When his father and uncle went back to China the following year, they took young Marco along with them.

The Polos sailed to Acre and probably traveled to China through Persia (Iran) and Afghanistan, following the ancient "Silk Road," a network of trading routes across mountains and deserts. They were welcomed by Kublai Khan, who, it is claimed, appointed Marco Polo as an official. He traveled widely in China and beyond, seeing many marvels. In 1292 the Polos escorted Kublai's daughter, the princess Kököchin, to Persia via Java. They arrived back in Venice in 1295. By 1300 a book about their travels was published. It may not always have contained the whole truth, but it did encourage later generations to dream of distant horizons.

In the Middle Ages, journeying could take a lifetime, and be full of dangers, adventures, setbacks, and delays—and wonderful sights in remote places. Ibn Battuta was probably one of the greatest of the Old World travelers— although as with Marco Polo, not all the details of his accounts are reliable.

Ibn Battuta (1304–69) was a Berber from Tangier, Morocco. The pilgrimage to Mecca was his first reason for leaving home at age 21. But he was in no hurry to return—it was about 30 years before he came home again! He was a likeable man who was fascinated by the people annd customs he encountered. Ibn Battutah traveled by boat, camel, horseback, and on foot. His routes took him through North Africa, Egypt, across Arabia, Turkey, and the Middle East, East Africa, Central Asia, India, and Sri Lanka and Southeast Asia. He may have even ventured as far as China, crossing the country and eventually reaching the capital Beijing itself.

1269	1271	1275	1292	1295	1325–27
Merchants Maffeo and Niccolò Polo return from a trading mission to Cathay (China).	The Polo brothers set out for China, taking along Niccolò's son Marco. They arrive in 1274.	Kublai Khan makes Marco Polo an official. Polo travels through China and beyond.	The Polos accompany a Chinese princess called Kököchin to her wedding in Persia.	Marco Polo returns to Venice, with many fine jewels.	Ibn Battuta sets out from Tangiers, visiting Cairo, Jerusalem, Medina, Mecca, Iraq and Persia.

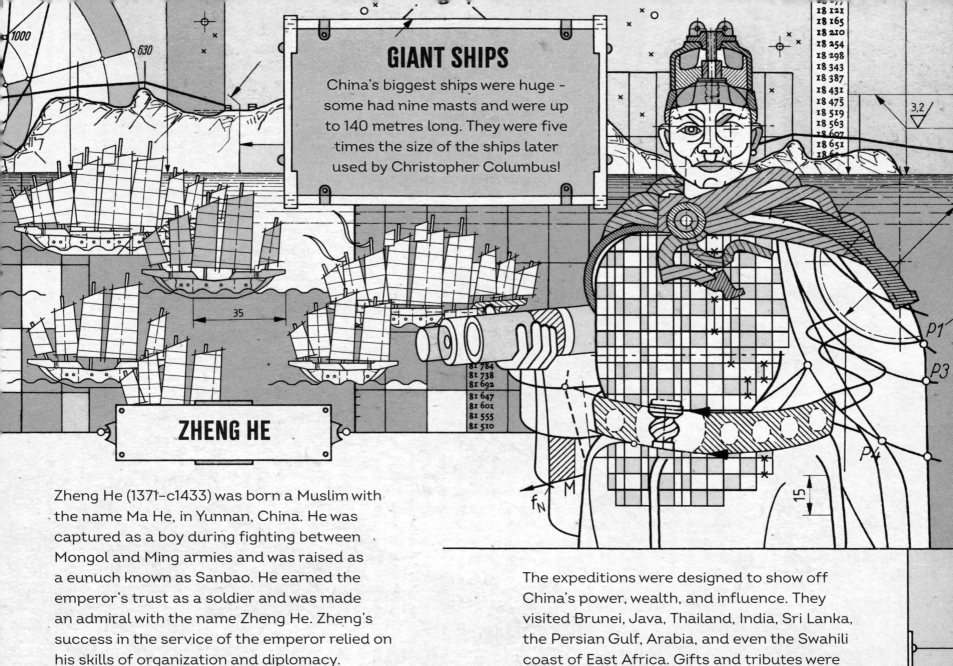

GIANT SHIPS

China's biggest ships were huge - some had nine masts and were up to 140 metres long. They were five times the size of the ships later used by Christopher Columbus!

ZHENG HE

Zheng He (1371–c1433) was born a Muslim with the name Ma He, in Yunnan, China. He was captured as a boy during fighting between Mongol and Ming armies and was raised as a eunuch known as Sanbao. He earned the emperor's trust as a soldier and was made an admiral with the name Zheng He. Zheng's success in the service of the emperor relied on his skills of organization and diplomacy.

Seafarers had been trading across the Indian Ocean since ancient times, but the seven Chinese expeditions to the "Western Oceans" between 1405 and 1433 were remarkable because of their size, probably the biggest in history. Zheng He's first voyage had a fleet of 317 ships, of which 62 were giant "treasure ships." These huge ships were the pride of the fleet. A ship's rudder excavated at Nanjing in 2015 was 33 feet high and weighed over 1,100 pounds. Zheng's ships made the ones later used by Christopher Columbus look like toys. Crew members numbered 28, 870.

The expeditions were designed to show off China's power, wealth, and influence. They visited Brunei, Java, Thailand, India, Sri Lanka, the Persian Gulf, Arabia, and even the Swahili coast of East Africa. Gifts and tributes were exchanged, such as gold, silver, silk, fine porcelain, and ivory. They also collected wild animals, including zebras, ostriches, and even giraffes—although not all survived the voyage home.

The Chinese had been leading the world in ship design for over a thousand years. They were the first to use rudders instead of steering oars, and they pioneered multiple masts and bulkheads (watertight compartments to reduce the risk of sinking if the ship takes on water). All these designs were eventually copied by the Europeans, along with some of the Chinese maps. Without these, the age of global exploration could never have started.

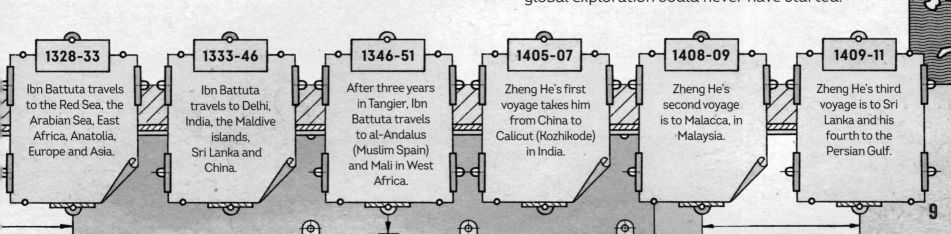

1328-33	1333-46	1346-51	1405-07	1408-09	1409-11
Ibn Battuta travels to the Red Sea, the Arabian Sea, East Africa, Anatolia, Europe and Asia.	Ibn Battuta travels to Delhi, India, the Maldive islands, Sri Lanka and China.	After three years in Tangier, Ibn Battuta travels to al-Andalus (Muslim Spain) and Mali in West Africa.	Zheng He's first voyage takes him from China to Calicut (Kozhikode) in India.	Zheng He's second voyage is to Malacca, in Malaysia.	Zheng He's third voyage is to Sri Lanka and his fourth to the Persian Gulf.

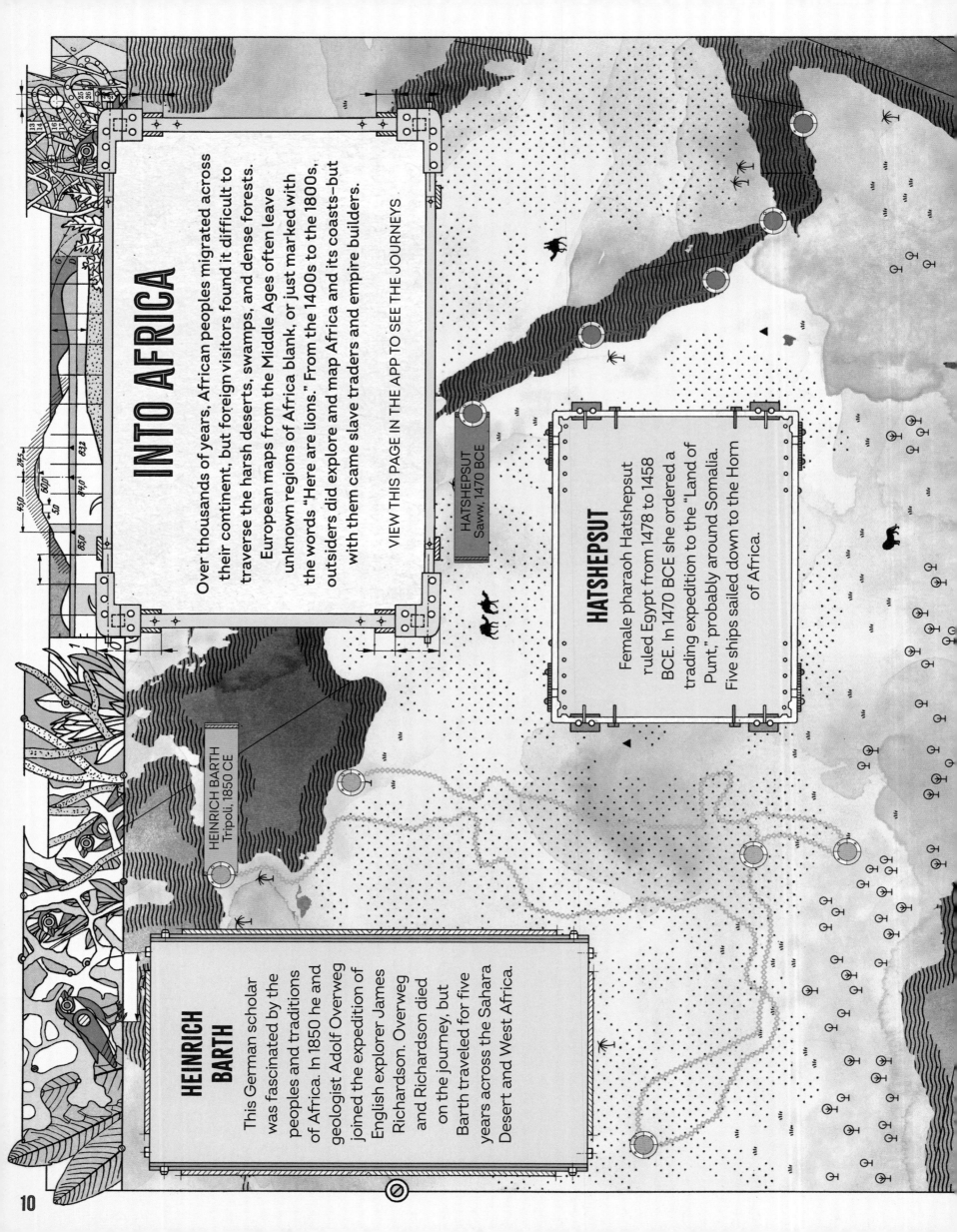

INTO AFRICA

Over thousands of years, African peoples migrated across their continent, but foreign visitors found it difficult to traverse the harsh deserts, swamps, and dense forests. European maps from the Middle Ages often leave unknown regions of Africa blank, or just marked with the words "Here are lions." From the 1400s to the 1800s, outsiders did explore and map Africa and its coasts—but with them came slave traders and empire builders.

VIEW THIS PAGE IN THE APP TO SEE THE JOURNEYS.

HATSHEPSUT
Saww, 1470 BCE

HATSHEPSUT

Female pharaoh Hatshepsut ruled Egypt from 1478 to 1458 BCE. In 1470 BCE she ordered a trading expedition to the "Land of Punt," probably around Somalia. Five ships sailed down to the Horn of Africa.

HEINRICH BARTH
Tripoli, 1850 CE

HEINRICH BARTH

This German scholar was fascinated by the peoples and traditions of Africa. In 1850 he and geologist Adolf Overweg joined the expedition of English explorer James Richardson. Overweg and Richardson died on the journey, but Barth traveled for five years across the Sahara Desert and West Africa.

DAVID LIVINGSTONE

In 1853, the famous Scottish missionary David Livingstone undertook a long journey in search of a passage from the west to the east coast of Africa, battling tropical illnesses and becoming cut off from the outside world.

DAVID LIVINGSTONE
Linyanti, 1853 CE

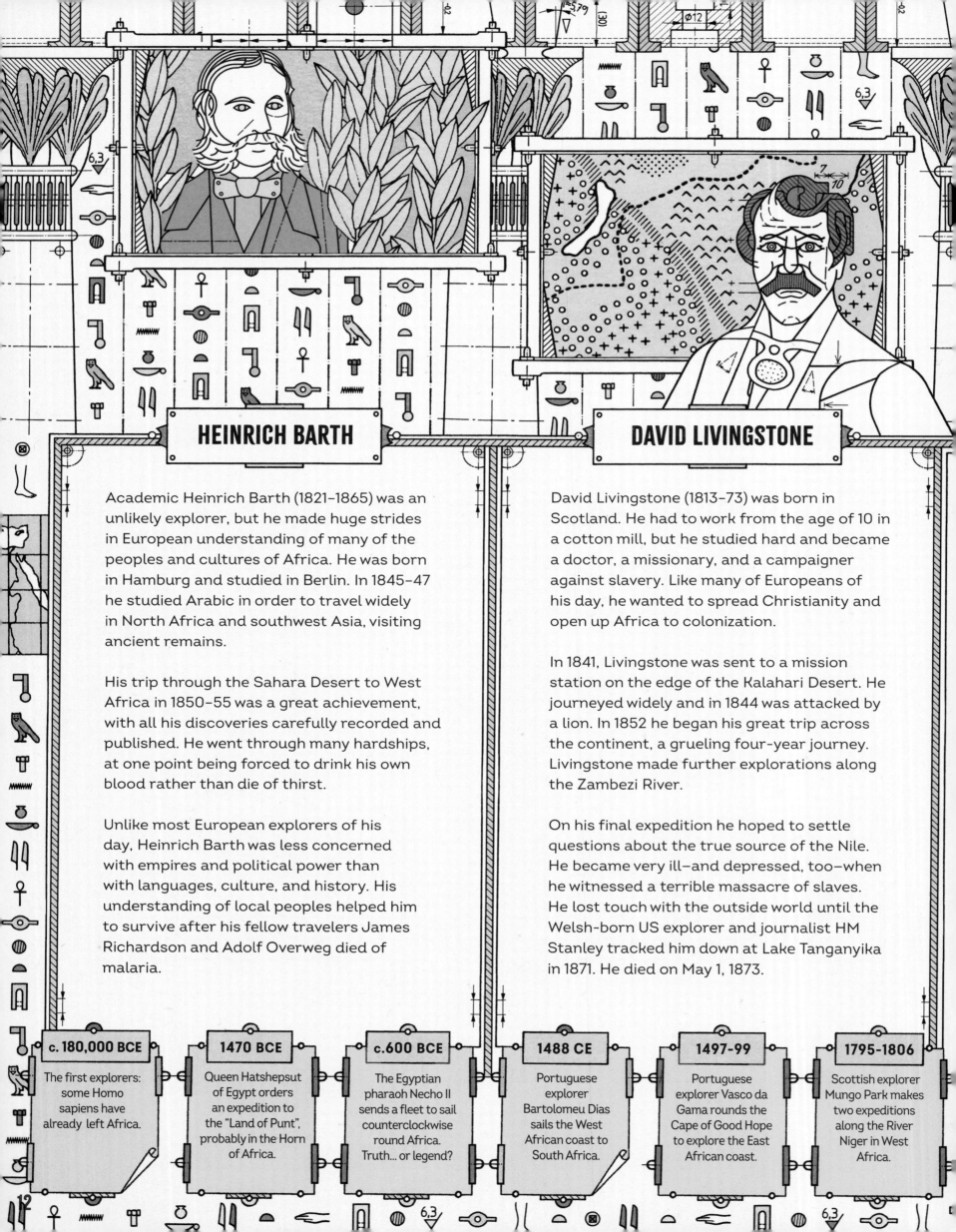

HEINRICH BARTH

Academic Heinrich Barth (1821–1865) was an unlikely explorer, but he made huge strides in European understanding of many of the peoples and cultures of Africa. He was born in Hamburg and studied in Berlin. In 1845–47 he studied Arabic in order to travel widely in North Africa and southwest Asia, visiting ancient remains.

His trip through the Sahara Desert to West Africa in 1850–55 was a great achievement, with all his discoveries carefully recorded and published. He went through many hardships, at one point being forced to drink his own blood rather than die of thirst.

Unlike most European explorers of his day, Heinrich Barth was less concerned with empires and political power than with languages, culture, and history. His understanding of local peoples helped him to survive after his fellow travelers James Richardson and Adolf Overweg died of malaria.

DAVID LIVINGSTONE

David Livingstone (1813–73) was born in Scotland. He had to work from the age of 10 in a cotton mill, but he studied hard and became a doctor, a missionary, and a campaigner against slavery. Like many of Europeans of his day, he wanted to spread Christianity and open up Africa to colonization.

In 1841, Livingstone was sent to a mission station on the edge of the Kalahari Desert. He journeyed widely and in 1844 was attacked by a lion. In 1852 he began his great trip across the continent, a grueling four-year journey. Livingstone made further explorations along the Zambezi River.

On his final expedition he hoped to settle questions about the true source of the Nile. He became very ill–and depressed, too–when he witnessed a terrible massacre of slaves. He lost touch with the outside world until the Welsh-born US explorer and journalist HM Stanley tracked him down at Lake Tanganyika in 1871. He died on May 1, 1873.

---

c. 180,000 BCE
The first explorers: some Homo sapiens have already left Africa.

1470 BCE
Queen Hatshepsut of Egypt orders an expedition to the "Land of Punt", probably in the Horn of Africa.

c.600 BCE
The Egyptian pharaoh Necho II sends a fleet to sail counterclockwise round Africa. Truth... or legend?

1488 CE
Portuguese explorer Bartolomeu Dias sails the West African coast to South Africa.

1497-99
Portuguese explorer Vasco da Gama rounds the Cape of Good Hope to explore the East African coast.

1795-1806
Scottish explorer Mungo Park makes two expeditions along the River Niger in West Africa.

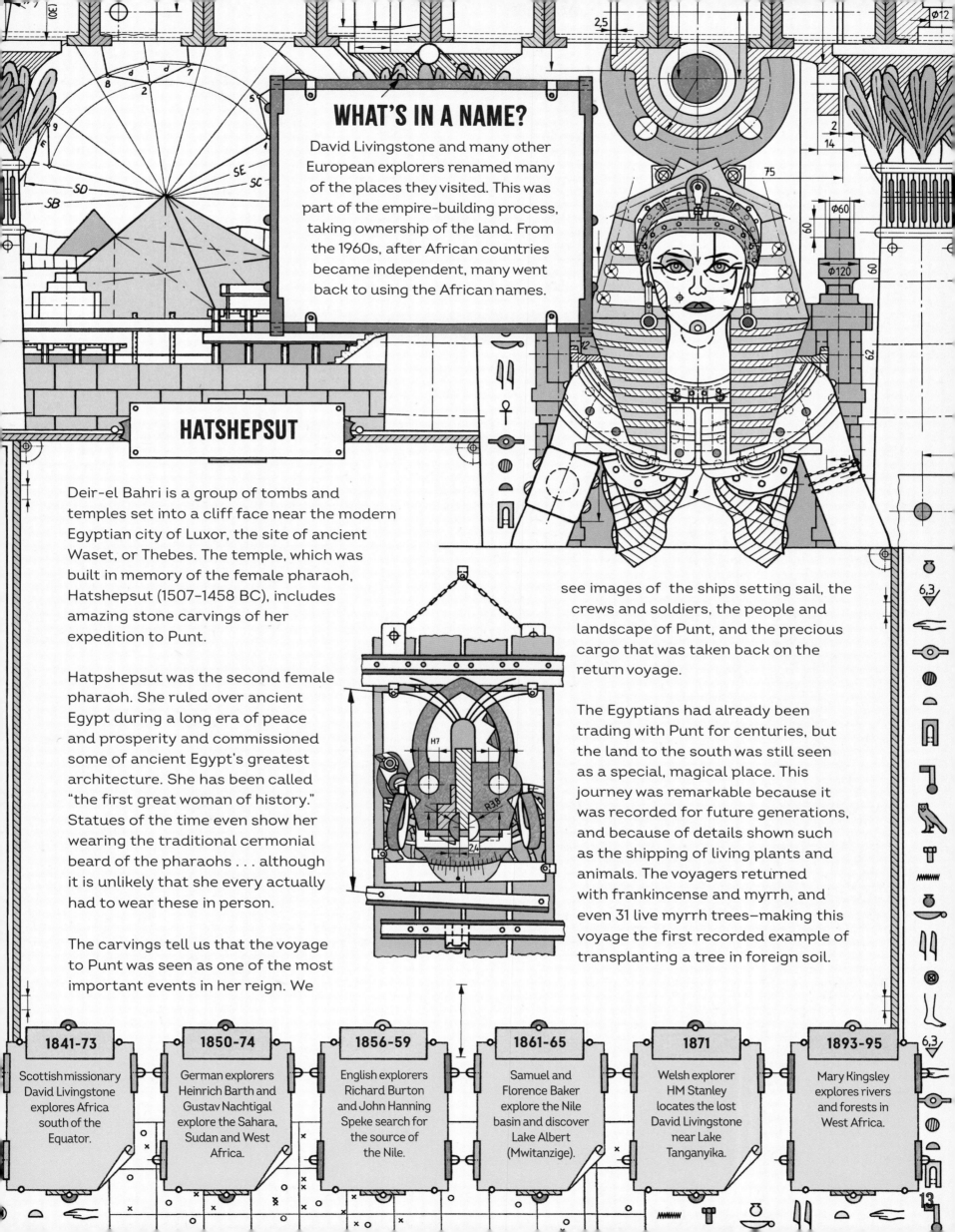

WHAT'S IN A NAME?

David Livingstone and many other European explorers renamed many of the places they visited. This was part of the empire-building process, taking ownership of the land. From the 1960s, after African countries became independent, many went back to using the African names.

HATSHEPSUT

Deir-el Bahri is a group of tombs and temples set into a cliff face near the modern Egyptian city of Luxor, the site of ancient Waset, or Thebes. The temple, which was built in memory of the female pharaoh, Hatshepsut (1507–1458 BC), includes amazing stone carvings of her expedition to Punt.

Hatpshepsut was the second female pharaoh. She ruled over ancient Egypt during a long era of peace and prosperity and commissioned some of ancient Egypt's greatest architecture. She has been called "the first great woman of history." Statues of the time even show her wearing the traditional cermonial beard of the pharaohs . . . although it is unlikely that she every actually had to wear these in person.

The carvings tell us that the voyage to Punt was seen as one of the most important events in her reign. We see images of the ships setting sail, the crews and soldiers, the people and landscape of Punt, and the precious cargo that was taken back on the return voyage.

The Egyptians had already been trading with Punt for centuries, but the land to the south was still seen as a special, magical place. This journey was remarkable because it was recorded for future generations, and because of details shown such as the shipping of living plants and animals. The voyagers returned with frankincense and myrrh, and even 31 live myrrh trees—making this voyage the first recorded example of transplanting a tree in foreign soil.

1841-73	1850-74	1856-59	1861-65	1871	1893-95
Scottish missionary David Livingstone explores Africa south of the Equator.	German explorers Heinrich Barth and Gustav Nachtigal explore the Sahara, Sudan and West Africa.	English explorers Richard Burton and John Hanning Speke search for the source of the Nile.	Samuel and Florence Baker explore the Nile basin and discover Lake Albert (Mwitanzige).	Welsh explorer HM Stanley locates the lost David Livingstone near Lake Tanganyika.	Mary Kingsley explores rivers and forests in West Africa.

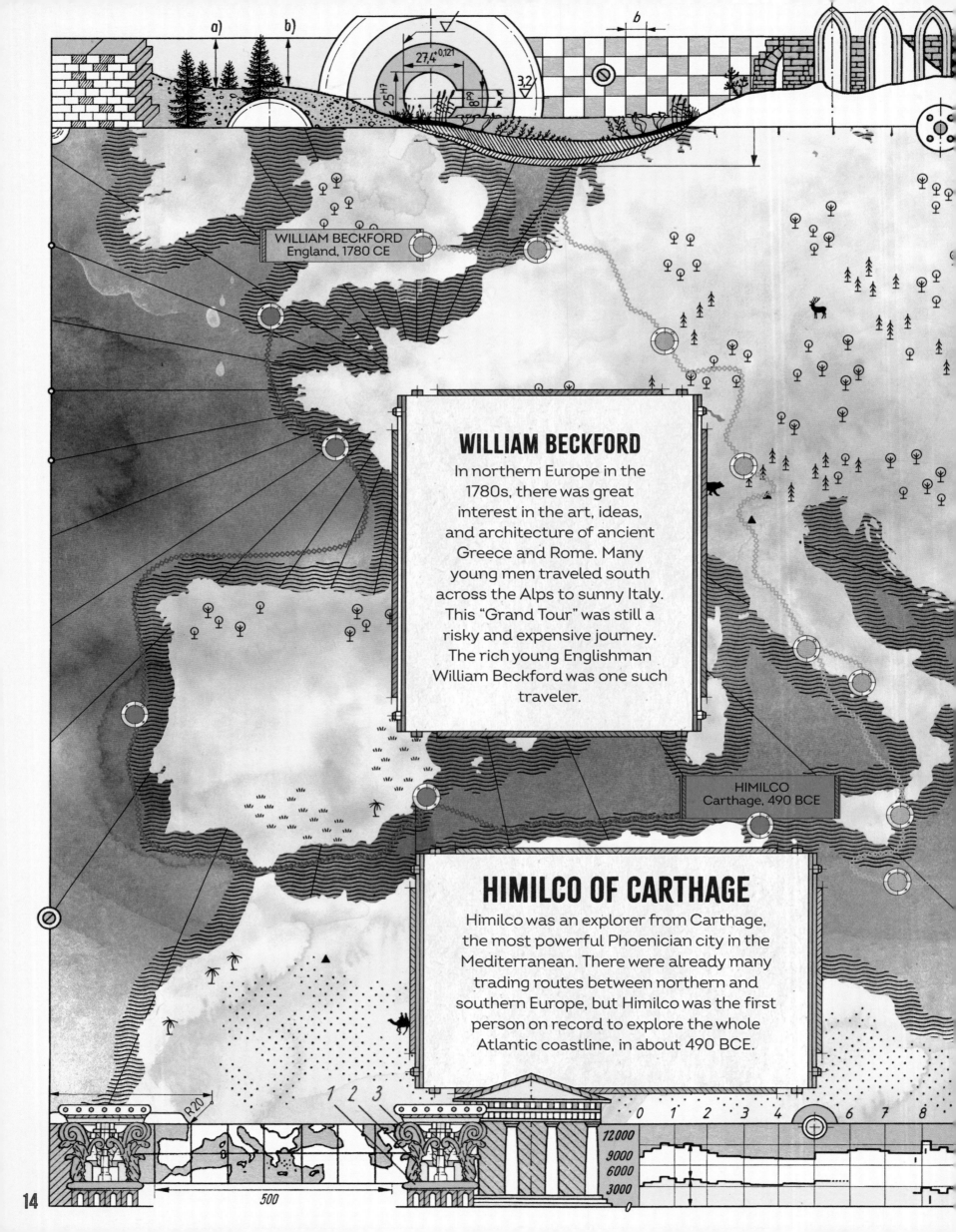

WILLIAM BECKFORD
England, 1780 CE

WILLIAM BECKFORD

In northern Europe in the 1780s, there was great interest in the art, ideas, and architecture of ancient Greece and Rome. Many young men traveled south across the Alps to sunny Italy. This "Grand Tour" was still a risky and expensive journey. The rich young Englishman William Beckford was one such traveler.

HIMILCO
Carthage, 490 BCE

HIMILCO OF CARTHAGE

Himilco was an explorer from Carthage, the most powerful Phoenician city in the Mediterranean. There were already many trading routes between northern and southern Europe, but Himilco was the first person on record to explore the whole Atlantic coastline, in about 490 BCE.

EXPLORING EUROPE

Humans began to explore Europe about 50,000 years ago, and since then, the continent has been criss-crossed with trade routes by both land and sea, from everyone from the ancient Minoans to the Romans and Vikings. But crossing Europe remained a dangerous occupation for history's travellers, even up to a few hundred years ago...

VIEW THIS PAGE IN THE APP TO SEE THE JOURNEYS

ST PAUL
Caesarea, 59 CE

SAINT PAUL

Saint Paul was one of the most famous voyagers in the early days of Christianity. In the first century CE, he made four great journeys around the Roman empire, risking shipwreck, bandits, deserts, and floods. Most of his travels were in Western Asia or Greece, but this last journey was to Rome itself.

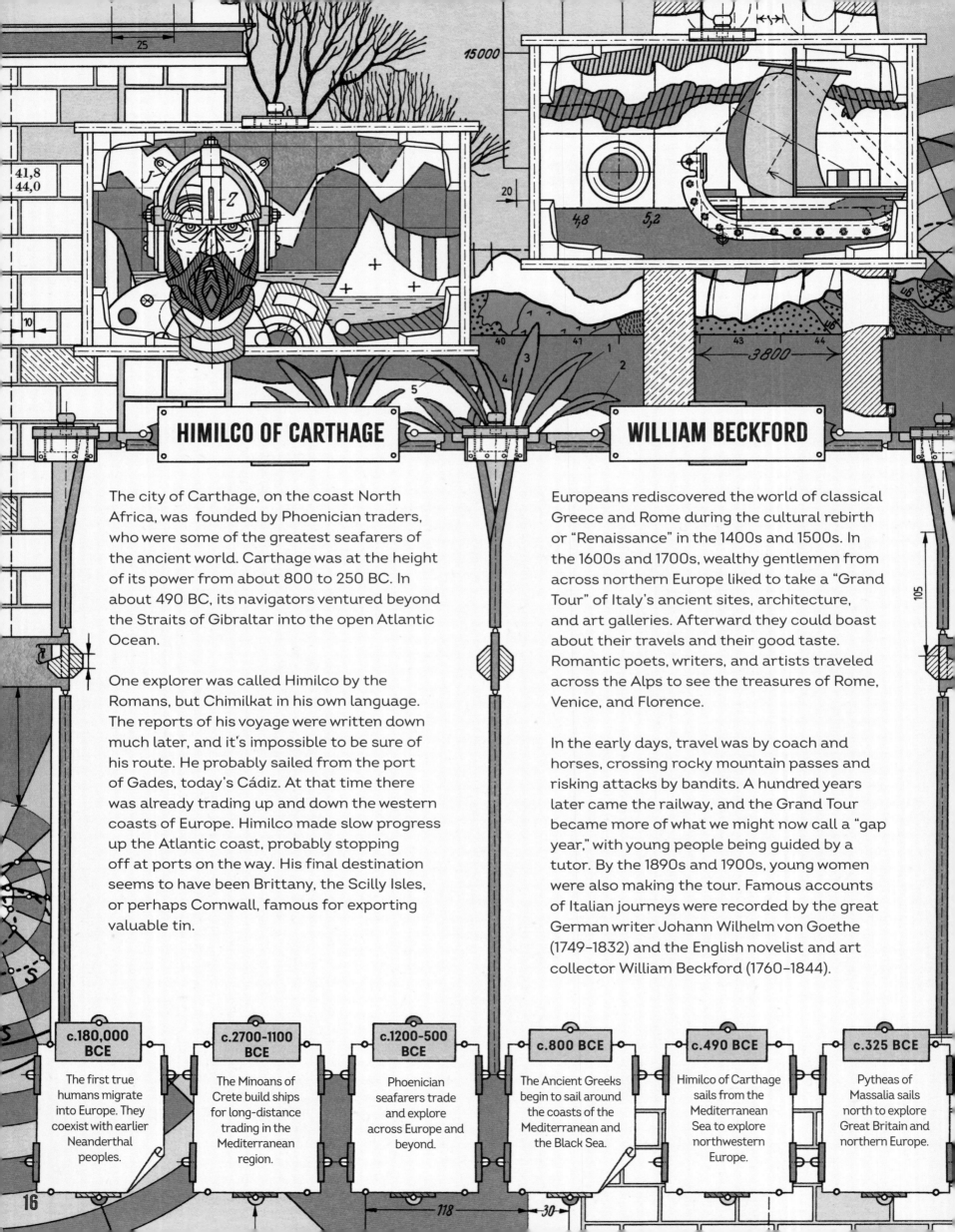

HIMILCO OF CARTHAGE

The city of Carthage, on the coast North Africa, was founded by Phoenician traders, who were some of the greatest seafarers of the ancient world. Carthage was at the height of its power from about 800 to 250 BC. In about 490 BC, its navigators ventured beyond the Straits of Gibraltar into the open Atlantic Ocean.

One explorer was called Himilco by the Romans, but Chimilkat in his own language. The reports of his voyage were written down much later, and it's impossible to be sure of his route. He probably sailed from the port of Gades, today's Cádiz. At that time there was already trading up and down the western coasts of Europe. Himilco made slow progress up the Atlantic coast, probably stopping off at ports on the way. His final destination seems to have been Brittany, the Scilly Isles, or perhaps Cornwall, famous for exporting valuable tin.

WILLIAM BECKFORD

Europeans rediscovered the world of classical Greece and Rome during the cultural rebirth or "Renaissance" in the 1400s and 1500s. In the 1600s and 1700s, wealthy gentlemen from across northern Europe liked to take a "Grand Tour" of Italy's ancient sites, architecture, and art galleries. Afterward they could boast about their travels and their good taste. Romantic poets, writers, and artists traveled across the Alps to see the treasures of Rome, Venice, and Florence.

In the early days, travel was by coach and horses, crossing rocky mountain passes and risking attacks by bandits. A hundred years later came the railway, and the Grand Tour became more of what we might now call a "gap year," with young people being guided by a tutor. By the 1890s and 1900s, young women were also making the tour. Famous accounts of Italian journeys were recorded by the great German writer Johann Wilhelm von Goethe (1749–1832) and the English novelist and art collector William Beckford (1760–1844).

c.180,000 BCE
The first true humans migrate into Europe. They coexist with earlier Neanderthal peoples.

c.2700–1100 BCE
The Minoans of Crete build ships for long-distance trading in the Mediterranean region.

c.1200–500 BCE
Phoenician seafarers trade and explore across Europe and beyond.

c.800 BCE
The Ancient Greeks begin to sail around the coasts of the Mediterranean and the Black Sea.

c.490 BCE
Himilco of Carthage sails from the Mediterranean Sea to explore northwestern Europe.

c.325 BCE
Pytheas of Massalia sails north to explore Great Britain and northern Europe.

ANCIENT TOURISTS

Tourism with an interest in history and art was already taking place about 2,000 years ago, when wealthy Greeks and Romans visited the ruins of Ancient Egypt. They even carved graffiti into the stones, some of which can still be seen today.

SAINT PAUL

Religion has always motivated people to travel, whether as pilgrims, scholars, or preachers of the faith. This has been true in many parts of the world. Hinduism spread from southern India to regions and islands in Southeast Asia. Buddhism opened up travel between India and China, and Japan and Central Asia. Islam spread from Arabia to many parts of Asia, Africa, and Europe.

The first great traveler in the name of the Christian faith was called Paul. *Paulus* is the Latin form of the Hebrew name Saul. Paul (c5–c64 CE) was a Jew from Tarsus in Cilicia (now southern Turkey). When he became a Christian, he wanted all peoples to join the new faith, whatever their ethnic or religious background. He made three great journeys through what is now Turkey and the Near East, Macedonia, and Greece. His fourth journey, as a prisoner, was to Rome. He also may have visited Spain. He is believed to have been executed and buried in Rome.

PYTHEAS

TALL TALES

Most of the early explorers told tales about their travels. Sometimes they–or other storytellers– exaggerated the details of the voyages with reports of gigantic sea monsters or evil spirits. Some historians suggest that Carthaginians such as Himilco intended to mislead other seafarers who might steal their trade.

c.500 BCE	c.240 BCE	c.125 CE	c.400 CE	c.790-1050	1648
Greek mathematician Pythagoras proposes that the Earth is a sphere.	Greek geographer Eratosthenes works out the Earth's circumference. He almost gets it right!	The Roman Empire expands its exploration, trade, conquest, and road building across Europe.	Decline of the Roman empire in the west, migrations of peoples across Europe.	Viking exploration, raiding, trading and exploration across Europe and beyond.	Peace between the Netherlands and Spain allows more Europeans to take the "Grand Tour" across Europe.

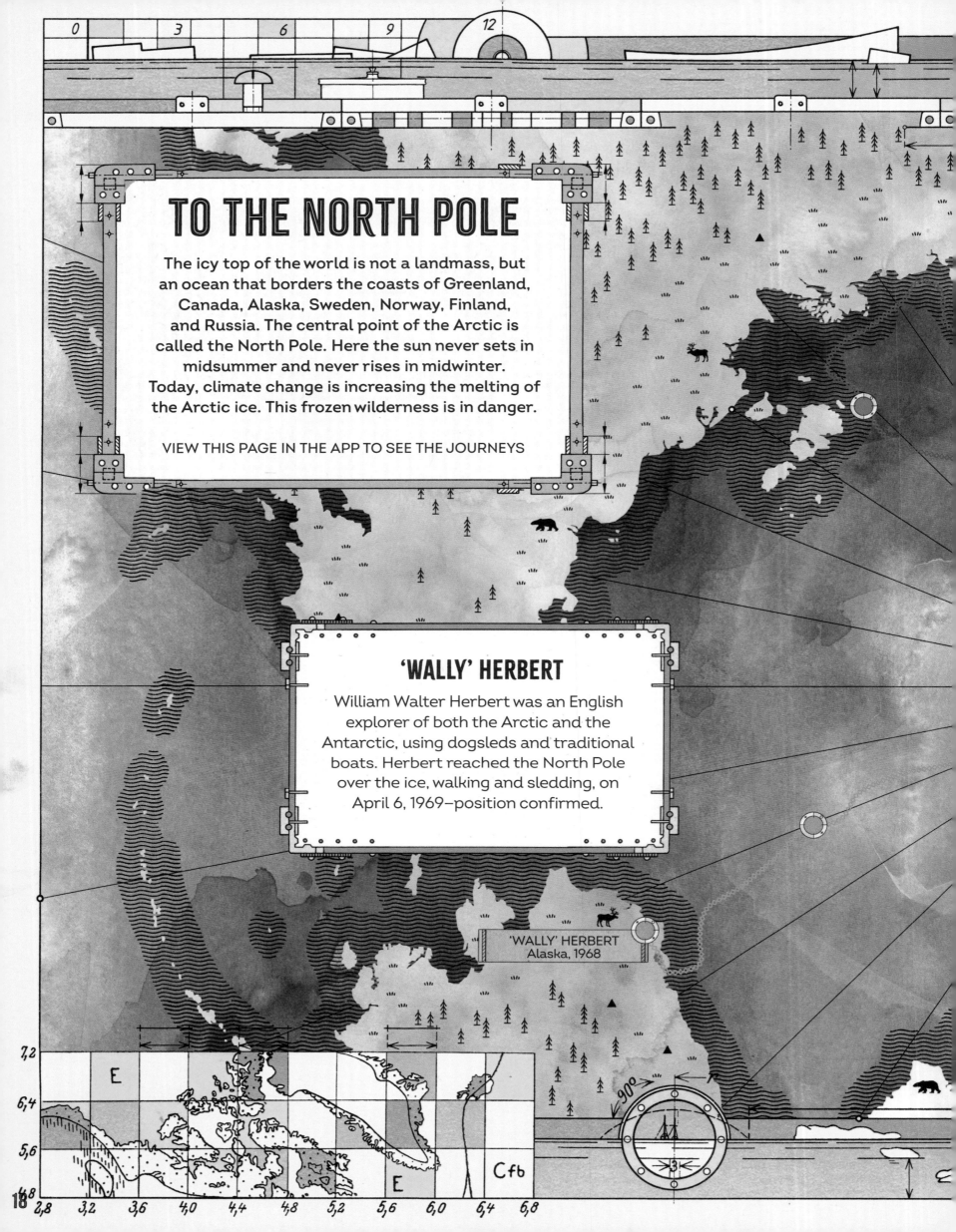

TO THE NORTH POLE

The icy top of the world is not a landmass, but an ocean that borders the coasts of Greenland, Canada, Alaska, Sweden, Norway, Finland, and Russia. The central point of the Arctic is called the North Pole. Here the sun never sets in midsummer and never rises in midwinter. Today, climate change is increasing the melting of the Arctic ice. This frozen wilderness is in danger.

VIEW THIS PAGE IN THE APP TO SEE THE JOURNEYS

'WALLY' HERBERT

William Walter Herbert was an English explorer of both the Arctic and the Antarctic, using dogsleds and traditional boats. Herbert reached the North Pole over the ice, walking and sledding, on April 6, 1969—position confirmed.

'WALLY' HERBERT
Alaska, 1968

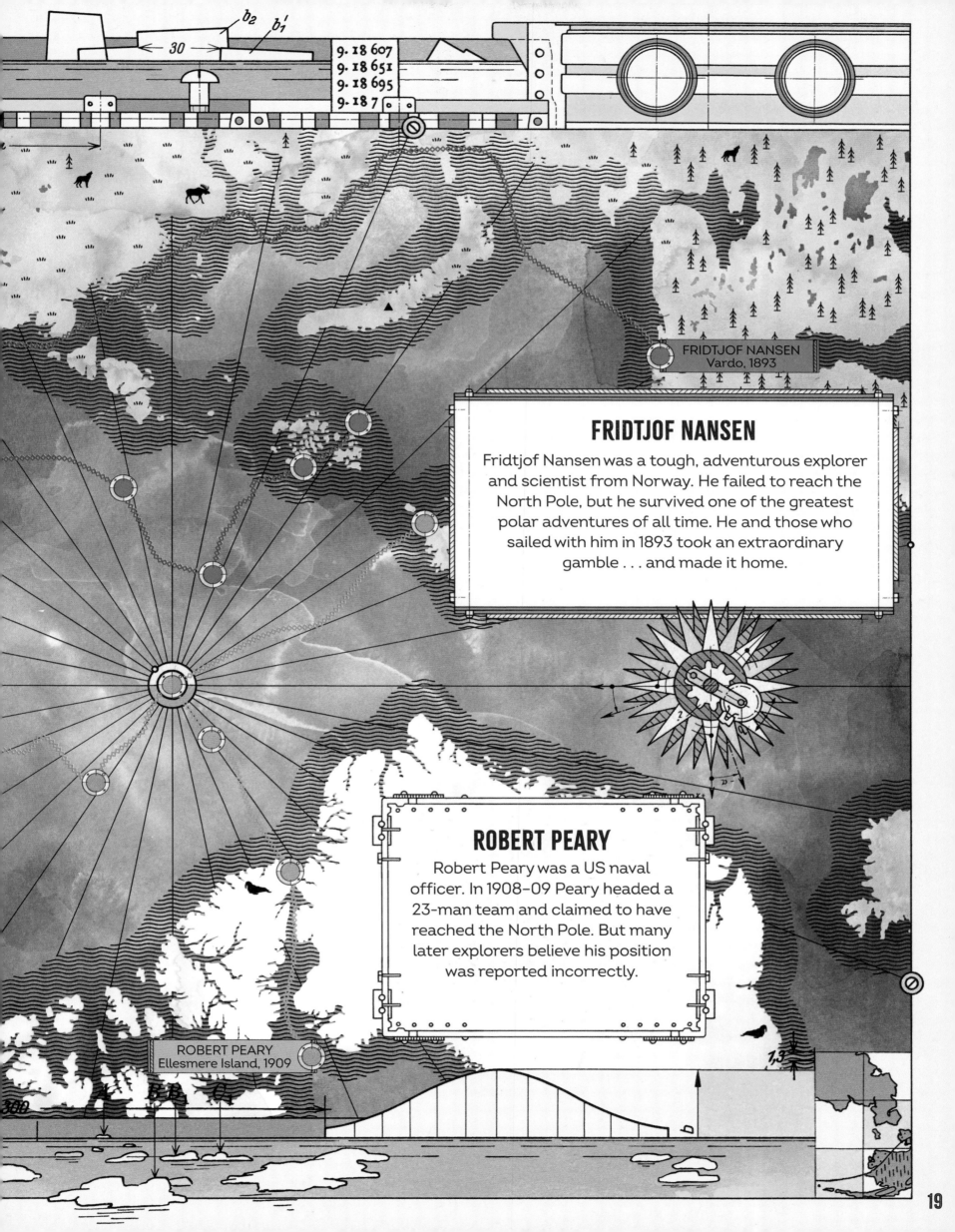

FRIDTJOF NANSEN
Vardo, 1893

FRIDTJOF NANSEN

Fridtjof Nansen was a tough, adventurous explorer and scientist from Norway. He failed to reach the North Pole, but he survived one of the greatest polar adventures of all time. He and those who sailed with him in 1893 took an extraordinary gamble . . . and made it home.

ROBERT PEARY

Robert Peary was a US naval officer. In 1908–09 Peary headed a 23-man team and claimed to have reached the North Pole. But many later explorers believe his position was reported incorrectly.

ROBERT PEARY
Ellesmere Island, 1909

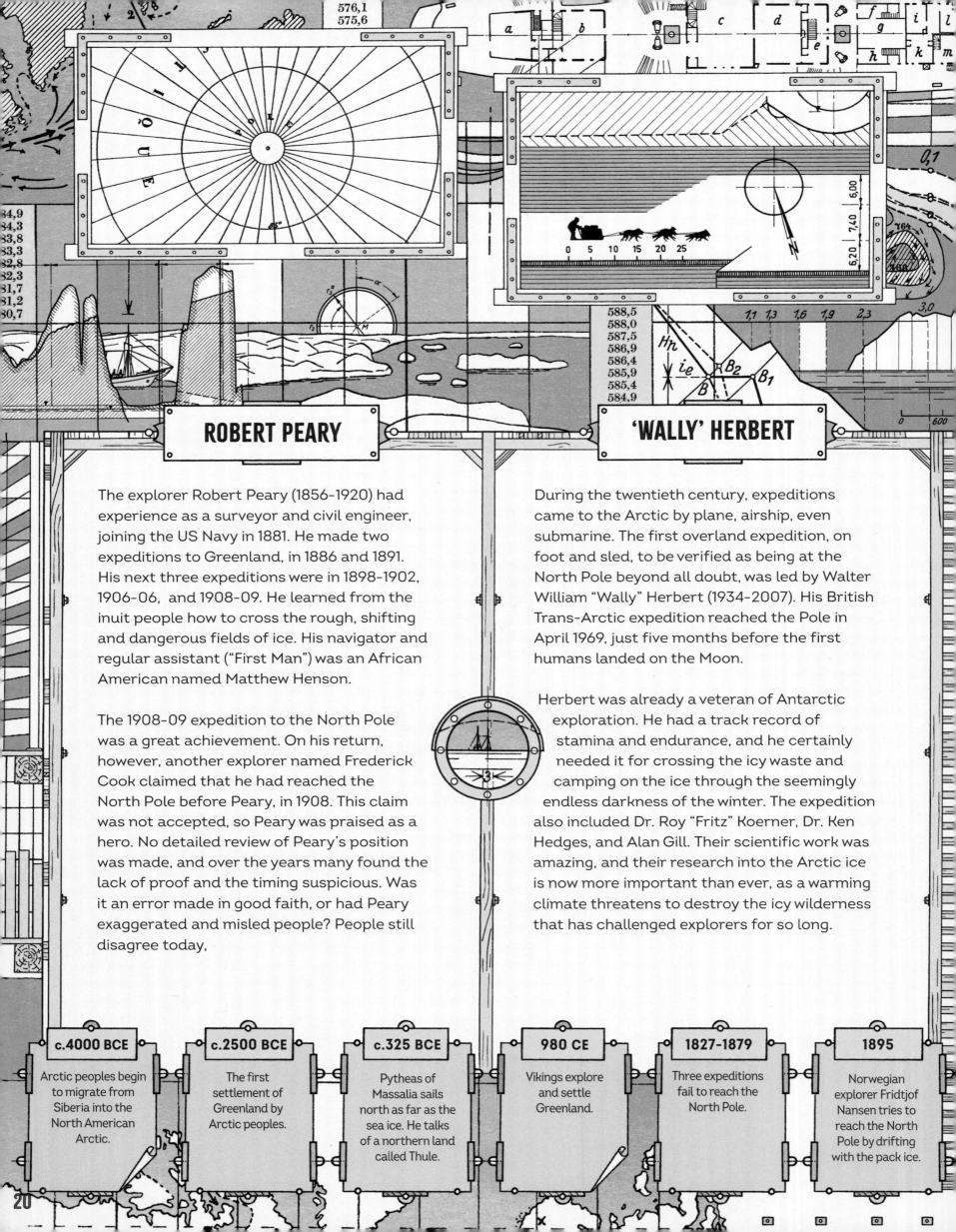

ROBERT PEARY

The explorer Robert Peary (1856-1920) had experience as a surveyor and civil engineer, joining the US Navy in 1881. He made two expeditions to Greenland, in 1886 and 1891. His next three expeditions were in 1898-1902, 1906-06, and 1908-09. He learned from the inuit people how to cross the rough, shifting and dangerous fields of ice. His navigator and regular assistant ("First Man") was an African American named Matthew Henson.

The 1908-09 expedition to the North Pole was a great achievement. On his return, however, another explorer named Frederick Cook claimed that he had reached the North Pole before Peary, in 1908. This claim was not accepted, so Peary was praised as a hero. No detailed review of Peary's position was made, and over the years many found the lack of proof and the timing suspicious. Was it an error made in good faith, or had Peary exaggerated and misled people? People still disagree today,

'WALLY' HERBERT

During the twentieth century, expeditions came to the Arctic by plane, airship, even submarine. The first overland expedition, on foot and sled, to be verified as being at the North Pole beyond all doubt, was led by Walter William "Wally" Herbert (1934-2007). His British Trans-Arctic expedition reached the Pole in April 1969, just five months before the first humans landed on the Moon.

Herbert was already a veteran of Antarctic exploration. He had a track record of stamina and endurance, and he certainly needed it for crossing the icy waste and camping on the ice through the seemingly endless darkness of the winter. The expedition also included Dr. Roy "Fritz" Koerner, Dr. Ken Hedges, and Alan Gill. Their scientific work was amazing, and their research into the Arctic ice is now more important than ever, as a warming climate threatens to destroy the icy wilderness that has challenged explorers for so long.

c.4000 BCE
Arctic peoples begin to migrate from Siberia into the North American Arctic.

c.2500 BCE
The first settlement of Greenland by Arctic peoples.

c.325 BCE
Pytheas of Massalia sails north as far as the sea ice. He talks of a northern land called Thule.

980 CE
Vikings explore and settle Greenland.

1827-1879
Three expeditions fail to reach the North Pole.

1895
Norwegian explorer Fridtjof Nansen tries to reach the North Pole by drifting with the pack ice.

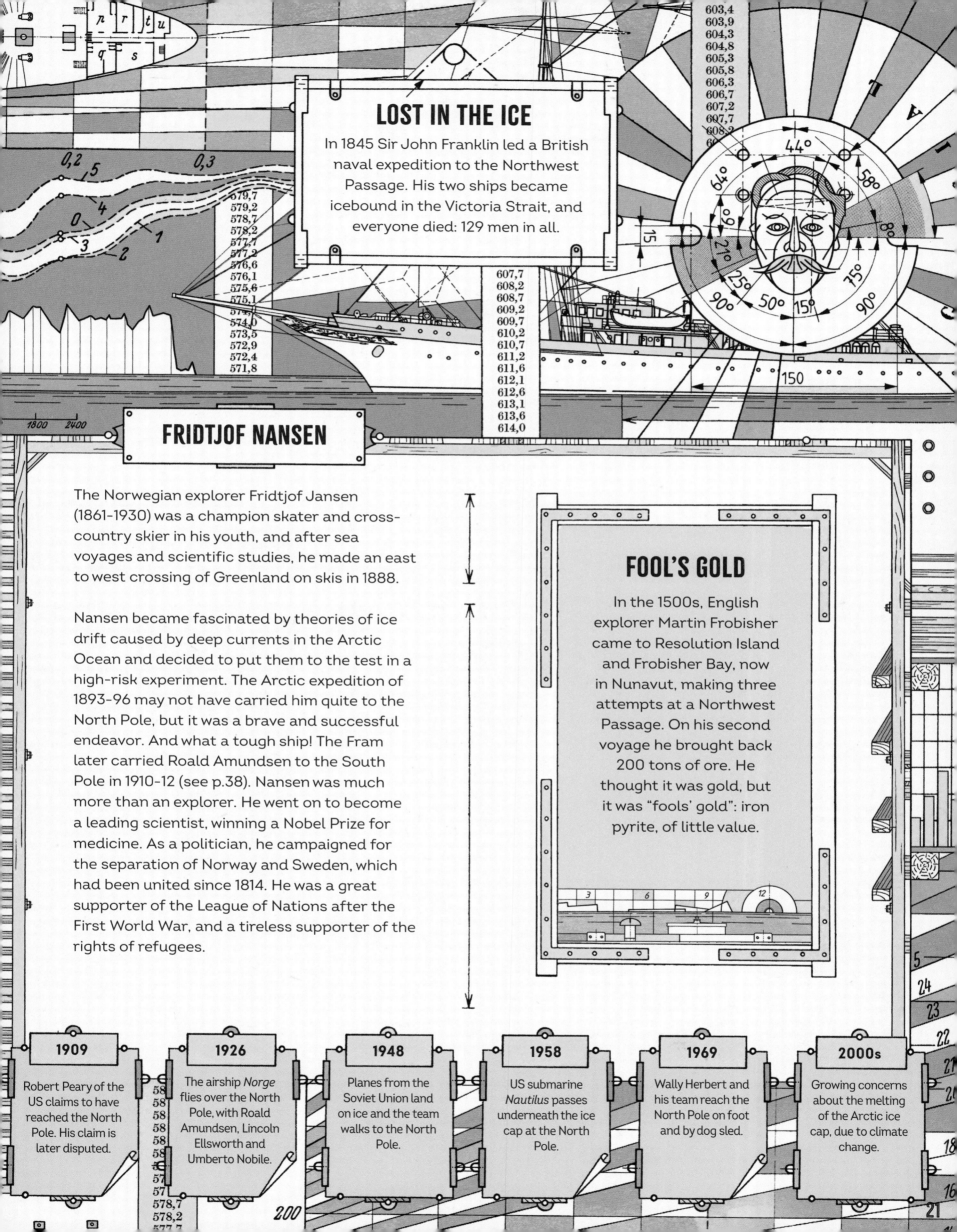

LOST IN THE ICE

In 1845 Sir John Franklin led a British naval expedition to the Northwest Passage. His two ships became icebound in the Victoria Strait, and everyone died: 129 men in all.

FRIDTJOF NANSEN

The Norwegian explorer Fridtjof Jansen (1861-1930) was a champion skater and cross-country skier in his youth, and after sea voyages and scientific studies, he made an east to west crossing of Greenland on skis in 1888.

Nansen became fascinated by theories of ice drift caused by deep currents in the Arctic Ocean and decided to put them to the test in a high-risk experiment. The Arctic expedition of 1893-96 may not have carried him quite to the North Pole, but it was a brave and successful endeavor. And what a tough ship! The Fram later carried Roald Amundsen to the South Pole in 1910-12 (see p.38). Nansen was much more than an explorer. He went on to become a leading scientist, winning a Nobel Prize for medicine. As a politician, he campaigned for the separation of Norway and Sweden, which had been united since 1814. He was a great supporter of the League of Nations after the First World War, and a tireless supporter of the rights of refugees.

FOOL'S GOLD

In the 1500s, English explorer Martin Frobisher came to Resolution Island and Frobisher Bay, now in Nunavut, making three attempts at a Northwest Passage. On his second voyage he brought back 200 tons of ore. He thought it was gold, but it was "fools' gold": iron pyrite, of little value.

1909
Robert Peary of the US claims to have reached the North Pole. His claim is later disputed.

1926
The airship *Norge* flies over the North Pole, with Roald Amundsen, Lincoln Ellsworth and Umberto Nobile.

1948
Planes from the Soviet Union land on ice and the team walks to the North Pole.

1958
US submarine *Nautilus* passes underneath the ice cap at the North Pole.

1969
Wally Herbert and his team reach the North Pole on foot and by dog sled.

2000s
Growing concerns about the melting of the Arctic ice cap, due to climate change.

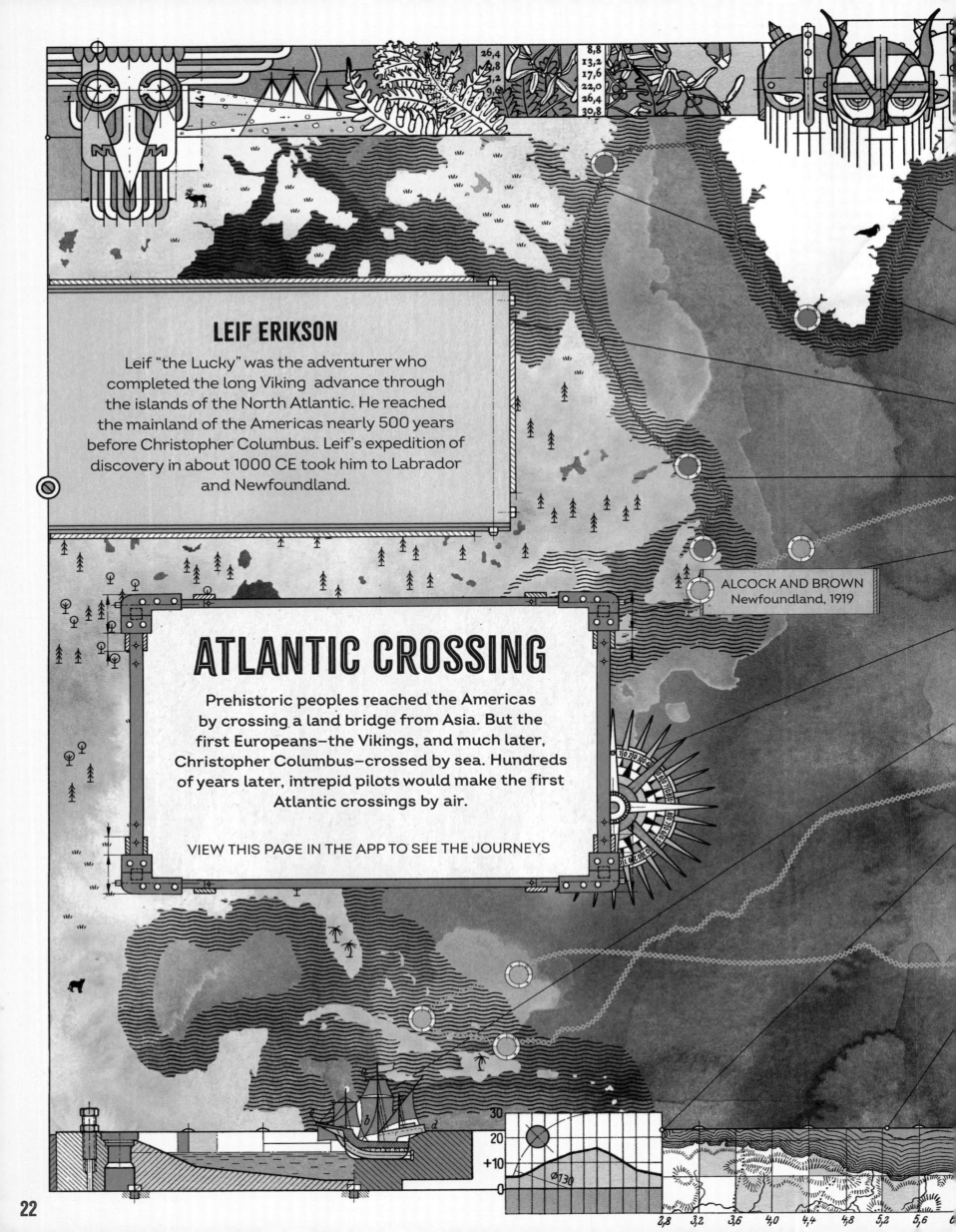

LEIF ERIKSON

Leif "the Lucky" was the adventurer who completed the long Viking advance through the islands of the North Atlantic. He reached the mainland of the Americas nearly 500 years before Christopher Columbus. Leif's expedition of discovery in about 1000 CE took him to Labrador and Newfoundland.

ALCOCK AND BROWN
Newfoundland, 1919

ATLANTIC CROSSING

Prehistoric peoples reached the Americas by crossing a land bridge from Asia. But the first Europeans—the Vikings, and much later, Christopher Columbus—crossed by sea. Hundreds of years later, intrepid pilots would make the first Atlantic crossings by air.

VIEW THIS PAGE IN THE APP TO SEE THE JOURNEYS

CHRISTOPHER COLUMBUS

Columbus was a skilled seafarer, but he is remembered chiefly as the man who introduced Europeans to the Americas. His discoveries changed the world forever, but to many the 1492 voyage of Columbus marks the start of Europe's scramble to control the New World, a period of ruthless greed, cruelty, and slavery.

CHRISTOPHER COLUMBUS
Palos de la Frontera, 1492

JOHN ALCOCK AND ARTHUR WHITTEN BROWN

British aviators John Alcock and Arthur Whitten Brown were the first to fly across the Atlantic Ocean nonstop, in June 1919. Their plane was a twin-engine Vickers Vimy biplane, originally designed for use as a bomber in World War I. The bombs racks were replaced by extra fuel tanks.

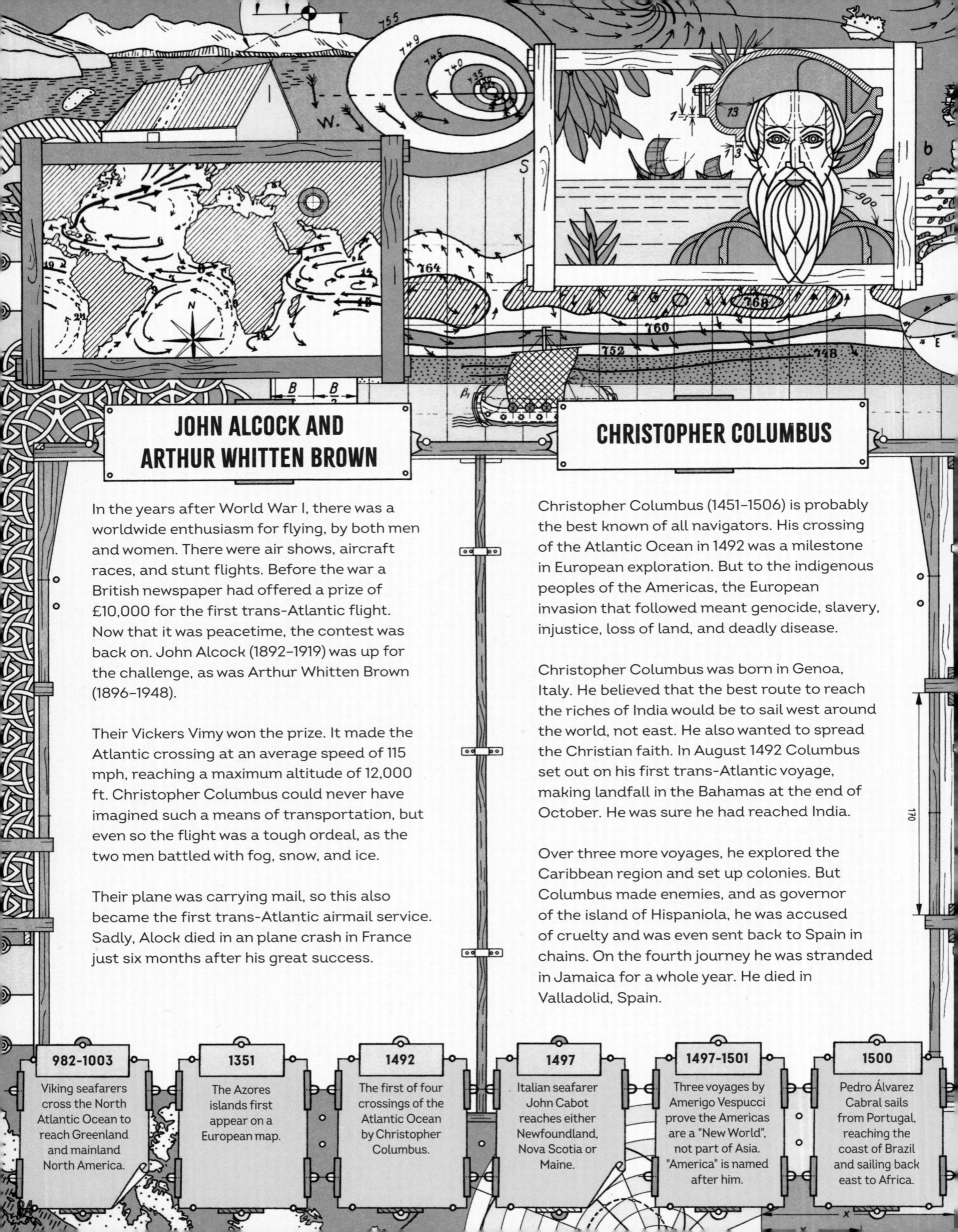

JOHN ALCOCK AND ARTHUR WHITTEN BROWN

In the years after World War I, there was a worldwide enthusiasm for flying, by both men and women. There were air shows, aircraft races, and stunt flights. Before the war a British newspaper had offered a prize of £10,000 for the first trans-Atlantic flight. Now that it was peacetime, the contest was back on. John Alcock (1892–1919) was up for the challenge, as was Arthur Whitten Brown (1896–1948).

Their Vickers Vimy won the prize. It made the Atlantic crossing at an average speed of 115 mph, reaching a maximum altitude of 12,000 ft. Christopher Columbus could never have imagined such a means of transportation, but even so the flight was a tough ordeal, as the two men battled with fog, snow, and ice.

Their plane was carrying mail, so this also became the first trans-Atlantic airmail service. Sadly, Alock died in an plane crash in France just six months after his great success.

CHRISTOPHER COLUMBUS

Christopher Columbus (1451–1506) is probably the best known of all navigators. His crossing of the Atlantic Ocean in 1492 was a milestone in European exploration. But to the indigenous peoples of the Americas, the European invasion that followed meant genocide, slavery, injustice, loss of land, and deadly disease.

Christopher Columbus was born in Genoa, Italy. He believed that the best route to reach the riches of India would be to sail west around the world, not east. He also wanted to spread the Christian faith. In August 1492 Columbus set out on his first trans-Atlantic voyage, making landfall in the Bahamas at the end of October. He was sure he had reached India.

Over three more voyages, he explored the Caribbean region and set up colonies. But Columbus made enemies, and as governor of the island of Hispaniola, he was accused of cruelty and was even sent back to Spain in chains. On the fourth journey he was stranded in Jamaica for a whole year. He died in Valladolid, Spain.

982-1003	1351	1492	1497	1497-1501	1500
Viking seafarers cross the North Atlantic Ocean to reach Greenland and mainland North America.	The Azores islands first appear on a European map.	The first of four crossings of the Atlantic Ocean by Christopher Columbus.	Italian seafarer John Cabot reaches either Newfoundland, Nova Scotia or Maine.	Three voyages by Amerigo Vespucci prove the Americas are a "New World", not part of Asia. "America" is named after him.	Pedro Álvarez Cabral sails from Portugal, reaching the coast of Brazil and sailing back east to Africa.

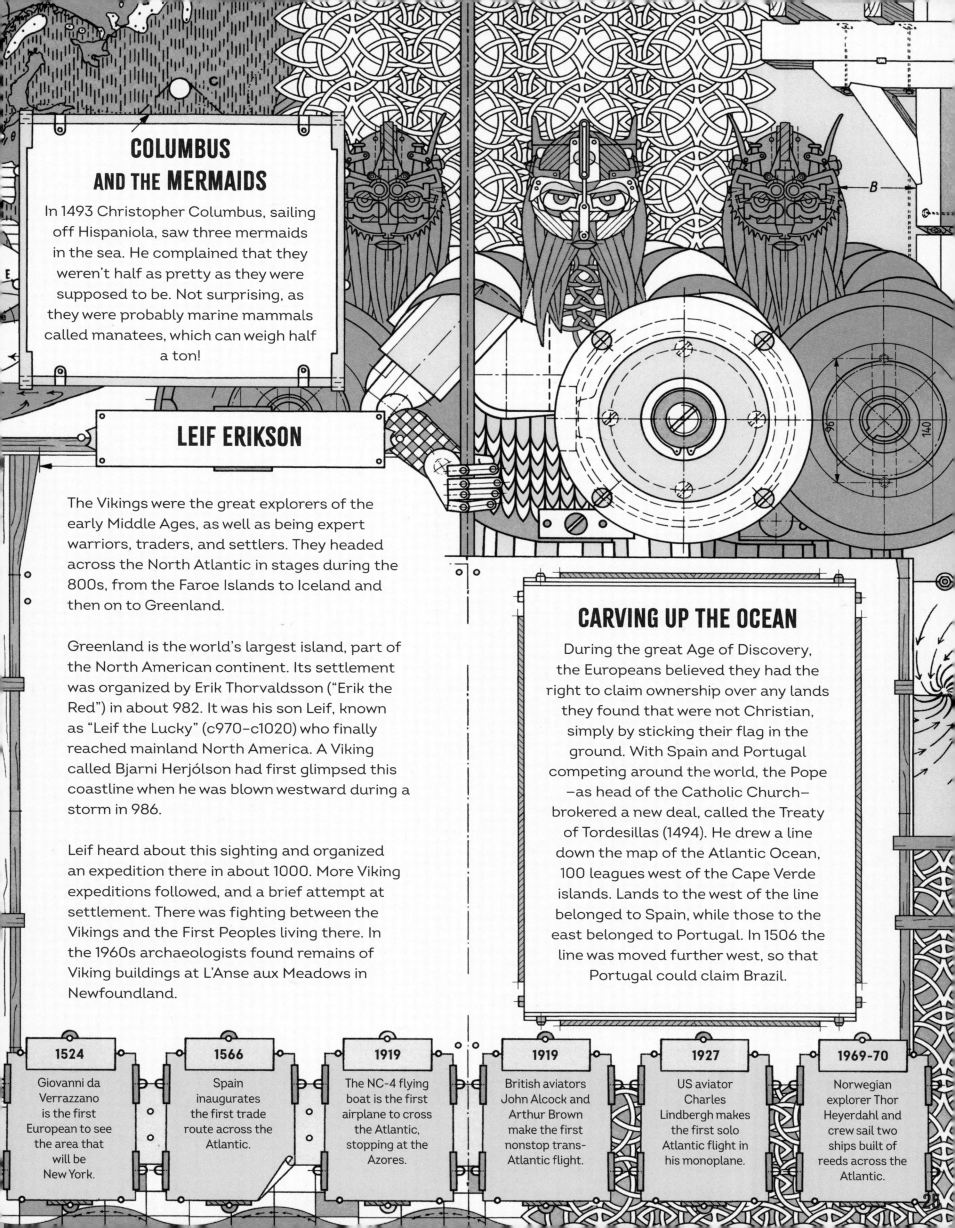

COLUMBUS AND THE MERMAIDS

In 1493 Christopher Columbus, sailing off Hispaniola, saw three mermaids in the sea. He complained that they weren't half as pretty as they were supposed to be. Not surprising, as they were probably marine mammals called manatees, which can weigh half a ton!

LEIF ERIKSON

The Vikings were the great explorers of the early Middle Ages, as well as being expert warriors, traders, and settlers. They headed across the North Atlantic in stages during the 800s, from the Faroe Islands to Iceland and then on to Greenland.

Greenland is the world's largest island, part of the North American continent. Its settlement was organized by Erik Thorvaldsson ("Erik the Red") in about 982. It was his son Leif, known as "Leif the Lucky" (c970–c1020) who finally reached mainland North America. A Viking called Bjarni Herjólson had first glimpsed this coastline when he was blown westward during a storm in 986.

Leif heard about this sighting and organized an expedition there in about 1000. More Viking expeditions followed, and a brief attempt at settlement. There was fighting between the Vikings and the First Peoples living there. In the 1960s archaeologists found remains of Viking buildings at L'Anse aux Meadows in Newfoundland.

CARVING UP THE OCEAN

During the great Age of Discovery, the Europeans believed they had the right to claim ownership over any lands they found that were not Christian, simply by sticking their flag in the ground. With Spain and Portugal competing around the world, the Pope –as head of the Catholic Church– brokered a new deal, called the Treaty of Tordesillas (1494). He drew a line down the map of the Atlantic Ocean, 100 leagues west of the Cape Verde islands. Lands to the west of the line belonged to Spain, while those to the east belonged to Portugal. In 1506 the line was moved further west, so that Portugal could claim Brazil.

1524	1566	1919	1919	1927	1969-70
Giovanni da Verrazzano is the first European to see the area that will be New York.	Spain inaugurates the first trade route across the Atlantic.	The NC-4 flying boat is the first airplane to cross the Atlantic, stopping at the Azores.	British aviators John Alcock and Arthur Brown make the first nonstop trans-Atlantic flight.	US aviator Charles Lindbergh makes the first solo Atlantic flight in his monoplane.	Norwegian explorer Thor Heyerdahl and crew sail two ships built of reeds across the Atlantic.

JUAN RODRÍGUEZ CABRILLO

The first European to navigate the coast of California, in 1542–43, was Juan Rodríguez Cabrillo. His fleet set out from the Spanish-conquered lands of Mexico and Central America, reaching the mouth of the Russian River in Northern California.

EXPLORING NORTH AMERICA

Prehistoric Asian peoples were North America's first explorers and settlers. European exploration began in the 1500s, displacing or destroying indigenous peoples and environments. The newcomers included fur traders, pioneers, and soldiers, as well as official navigators and mapmakers.

VIEW THIS PAGE IN THE APP
TO SEE THE JOURNEYS

JUAN RODRÍGUEZ
CABRILLO
Baja California, 1542

MERIWETHER LEWIS AND WILLIAM CLARK

In 1803 the United States purchased France's huge 1,329,734 sq. mi. North American territory. An exploratory mission was led by Meriwether Lewis and William Clark, assisted by a Shoshone woman called Sacagawea.

MERIWETHER LEWIS AND WILLIAM CLARK
St Louis, 1804

HERNANDO DE SOTO

Hernando de Soto was a Spanish soldier and adventurer. His best-known expedition (1539–1542) went north to the Appalachian Mountains, then west across the Mississippi, in search of gold he would never find.

HERNANDO DE SOTO
Havana, 1539

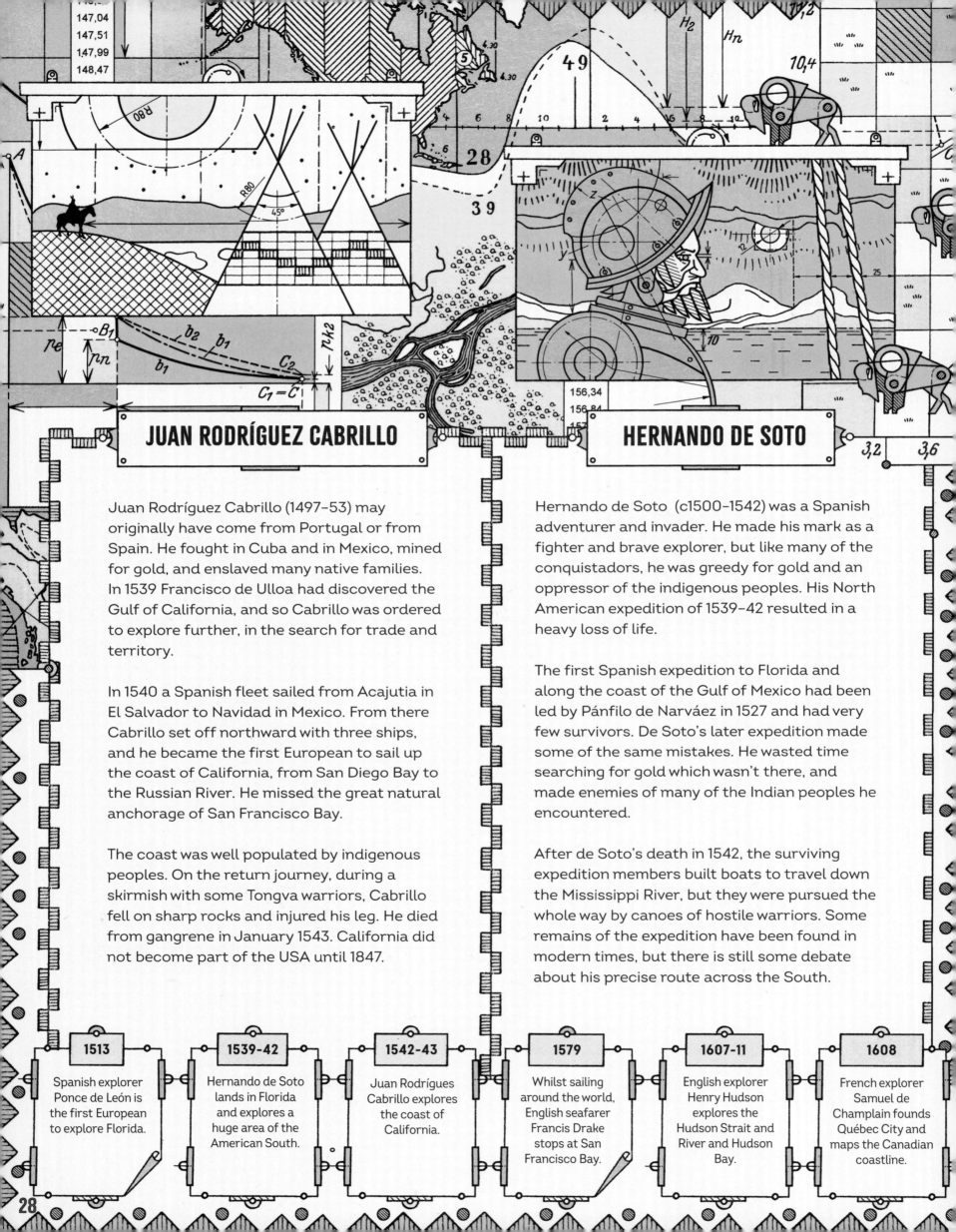

JUAN RODRÍGUEZ CABRILLO

HERNANDO DE SOTO

Juan Rodríguez Cabrillo (1497–53) may originally have come from Portugal or from Spain. He fought in Cuba and in Mexico, mined for gold, and enslaved many native families. In 1539 Francisco de Ulloa had discovered the Gulf of California, and so Cabrillo was ordered to explore further, in the search for trade and territory.

In 1540 a Spanish fleet sailed from Acajutia in El Salvador to Navidad in Mexico. From there Cabrillo set off northward with three ships, and he became the first European to sail up the coast of California, from San Diego Bay to the Russian River. He missed the great natural anchorage of San Francisco Bay.

The coast was well populated by indigenous peoples. On the return journey, during a skirmish with some Tongva warriors, Cabrillo fell on sharp rocks and injured his leg. He died from gangrene in January 1543. California did not become part of the USA until 1847.

Hernando de Soto (c1500–1542) was a Spanish adventurer and invader. He made his mark as a fighter and brave explorer, but like many of the conquistadors, he was greedy for gold and an oppressor of the indigenous peoples. His North American expedition of 1539–42 resulted in a heavy loss of life.

The first Spanish expedition to Florida and along the coast of the Gulf of Mexico had been led by Pánfilo de Narváez in 1527 and had very few survivors. De Soto's later expedition made some of the same mistakes. He wasted time searching for gold which wasn't there, and made enemies of many of the Indian peoples he encountered.

After de Soto's death in 1542, the surviving expedition members built boats to travel down the Mississippi River, but they were pursued the whole way by canoes of hostile warriors. Some remains of the expedition have been found in modern times, but there is still some debate about his precise route across the South.

1513
Spanish explorer Ponce de León is the first European to explore Florida.

1539–42
Hernando de Soto lands in Florida and explores a huge area of the American South.

1542–43
Juan Rodrígues Cabrillo explores the coast of California.

1579
Whilst sailing around the world, English seafarer Francis Drake stops at San Francisco Bay.

1607–11
English explorer Henry Hudson explores the Hudson Strait and River and Hudson Bay.

1608
French explorer Samuel de Champlain founds Québec City and maps the Canadian coastline.

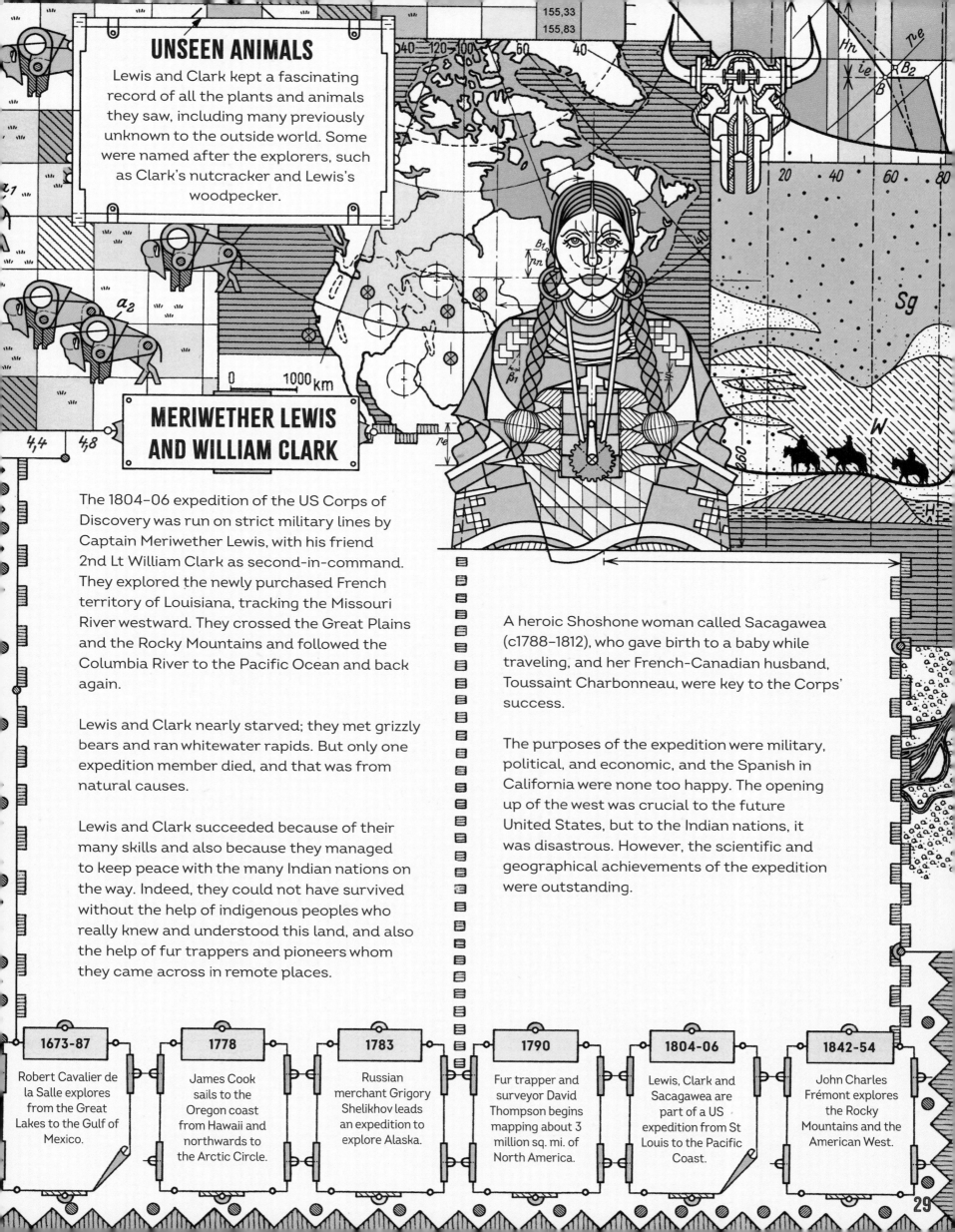

UNSEEN ANIMALS

Lewis and Clark kept a fascinating record of all the plants and animals they saw, including many previously unknown to the outside world. Some were named after the explorers, such as Clark's nutcracker and Lewis's woodpecker.

MERIWETHER LEWIS AND WILLIAM CLARK

The 1804–06 expedition of the US Corps of Discovery was run on strict military lines by Captain Meriwether Lewis, with his friend 2nd Lt William Clark as second-in-command. They explored the newly purchased French territory of Louisiana, tracking the Missouri River westward. They crossed the Great Plains and the Rocky Mountains and followed the Columbia River to the Pacific Ocean and back again.

Lewis and Clark nearly starved; they met grizzly bears and ran whitewater rapids. But only one expedition member died, and that was from natural causes.

Lewis and Clark succeeded because of their many skills and also because they managed to keep peace with the many Indian nations on the way. Indeed, they could not have survived without the help of indigenous peoples who really knew and understood this land, and also the help of fur trappers and pioneers whom they came across in remote places.

A heroic Shoshone woman called Sacagawea (c1788–1812), who gave birth to a baby while traveling, and her French-Canadian husband, Toussaint Charbonneau, were key to the Corps' success.

The purposes of the expedition were military, political, and economic, and the Spanish in California were none too happy. The opening up of the west was crucial to the future United States, but to the Indian nations, it was disastrous. However, the scientific and geographical achievements of the expedition were outstanding.

1673-87
Robert Cavalier de la Salle explores from the Great Lakes to the Gulf of Mexico.

1778
James Cook sails to the Oregon coast from Hawaii and northwards to the Arctic Circle.

1783
Russian merchant Grigory Shelikhov leads an expedition to explore Alaska.

1790
Fur trapper and surveyor David Thompson begins mapping about 3 million sq. mi. of North America.

1804-06
Lewis, Clark and Sacagawea are part of a US expedition from St Louis to the Pacific Coast.

1842-54
John Charles Frémont explores the Rocky Mountains and the American West.

CENTRAL AND SOUTH AMERICA

Over tens of thousands of years, migrating peoples explored Central and South America. Great cities and civilizations grew up in what is now Mexico and Peru. Polynesian explorers or traders may have reached South America's Pacific Coast long ago, before Europeans discovered and invaded the continent in the 1500s. These brutal conquistadors came in search of gold and land, but later explorers came as mapmakers, or as scientists researching geology and evolution.

VIEW THIS PAGE IN THE APP TO SEE THE JOURNEYS

CHARLES DARWIN
Salvador, 1831

ALEXANDER VON HUMBOLDT
Cumaná, 1799

FRANCISCO DE ORELLANA
Quito, 1541

ALEXANDER VON HUMBOLDT

Prussian scientist and geographer Alexander von Humboldt explored Venezuela, Cuba, Colombia, Ecuador, and Mexico, studying climate, mapmaking, plants, animals, geology, history, and cultures.

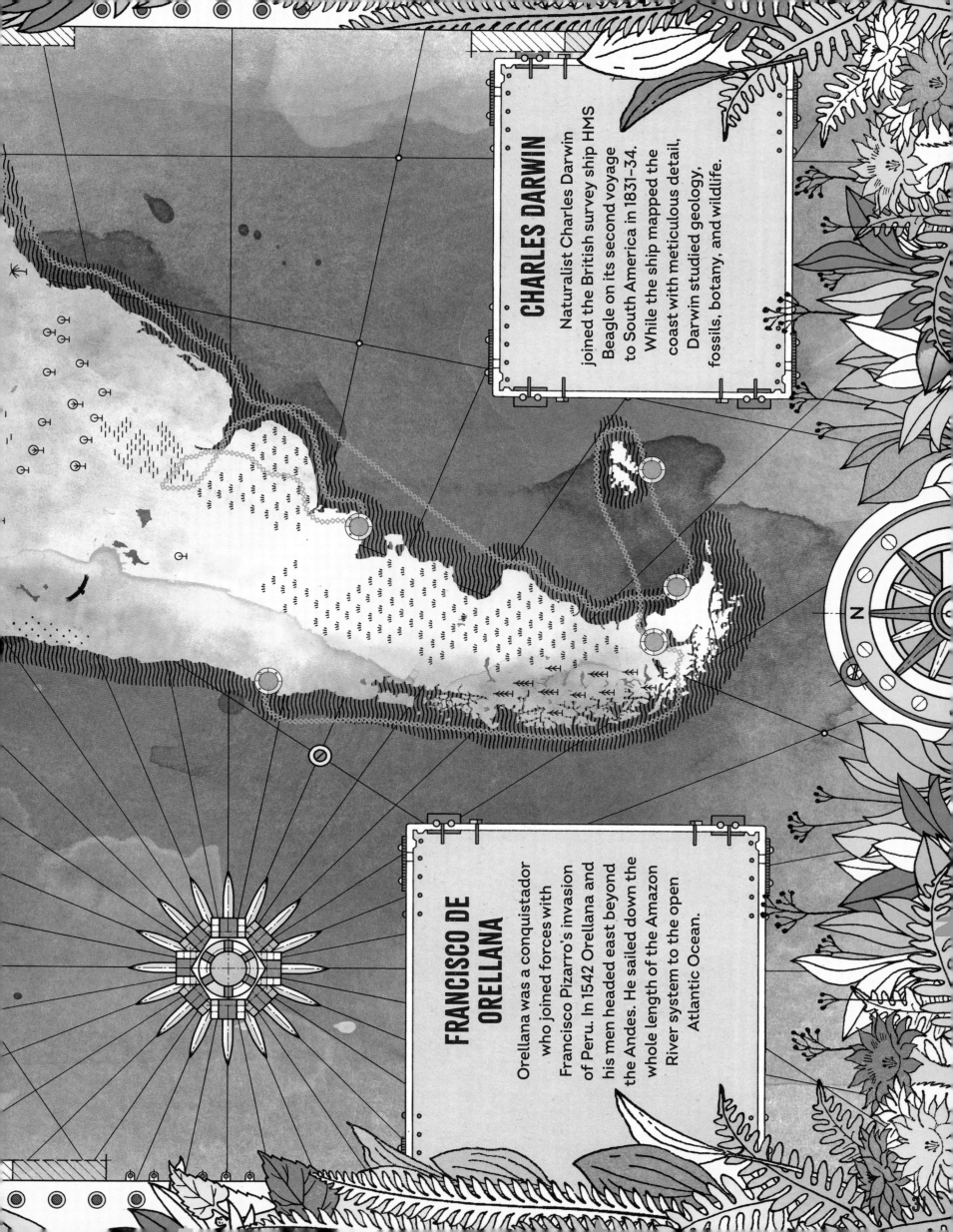

CHARLES DARWIN

Naturalist Charles Darwin joined the British survey ship HMS Beagle on its second voyage to South America in 1831–34. While the ship mapped the coast with meticulous detail, Darwin studied geology, fossils, botany, and wildlife.

FRANCISCO DE ORELLANA

Orellana was a conquistador who joined forces with Francisco Pizarro's invasion of Peru. In 1542 Orellana and his men headed east beyond the Andes. He sailed down the whole length of the Amazon River system to the open Atlantic Ocean.

N

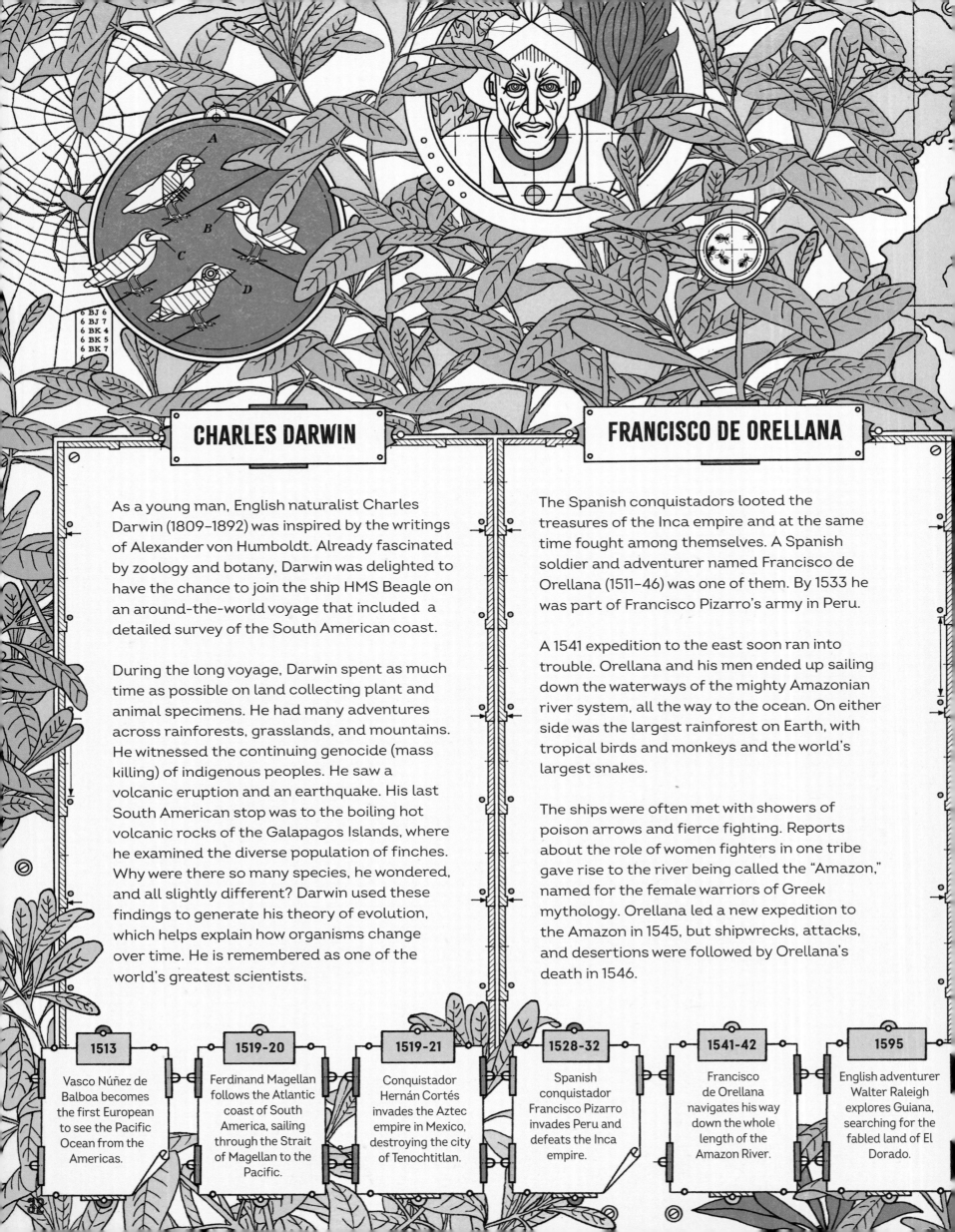

CHARLES DARWIN

As a young man, English naturalist Charles Darwin (1809–1892) was inspired by the writings of Alexander von Humboldt. Already fascinated by zoology and botany, Darwin was delighted to have the chance to join the ship HMS Beagle on an around-the-world voyage that included a detailed survey of the South American coast.

During the long voyage, Darwin spent as much time as possible on land collecting plant and animal specimens. He had many adventures across rainforests, grasslands, and mountains. He witnessed the continuing genocide (mass killing) of indigenous peoples. He saw a volcanic eruption and an earthquake. His last South American stop was to the boiling hot volcanic rocks of the Galapagos Islands, where he examined the diverse population of finches. Why were there so many species, he wondered, and all slightly different? Darwin used these findings to generate his theory of evolution, which helps explain how organisms change over time. He is remembered as one of the world's greatest scientists.

FRANCISCO DE ORELLANA

The Spanish conquistadors looted the treasures of the Inca empire and at the same time fought among themselves. A Spanish soldier and adventurer named Francisco de Orellana (1511–46) was one of them. By 1533 he was part of Francisco Pizarro's army in Peru.

A 1541 expedition to the east soon ran into trouble. Orellana and his men ended up sailing down the waterways of the mighty Amazonian river system, all the way to the ocean. On either side was the largest rainforest on Earth, with tropical birds and monkeys and the world's largest snakes.

The ships were often met with showers of poison arrows and fierce fighting. Reports about the role of women fighters in one tribe gave rise to the river being called the "Amazon," named for the female warriors of Greek mythology. Orellana led a new expedition to the Amazon in 1545, but shipwrecks, attacks, and desertions were followed by Orellana's death in 1546.

1513

Vasco Núñez de Balboa becomes the first European to see the Pacific Ocean from the Americas.

1519–20

Ferdinand Magellan follows the Atlantic coast of South America, sailing through the Strait of Magellan to the Pacific.

1519–21

Conquistador Hernán Cortés invades the Aztec empire in Mexico, destroying the city of Tenochtitlan.

1528–32

Spanish conquistador Francisco Pizarro invades Peru and defeats the Inca empire.

1541–42

Francisco de Orellana navigates his way down the whole length of the Amazon River.

1595

English adventurer Walter Raleigh explores Guiana, searching for the fabled land of El Dorado.

FABLES OF EL DORADO

Many explorers were driven by the search for gold. A false rumor grew up of a native chief so wealthy that he was covered in gold dust. In Spanish he was known as El Dorado, "the Golden One."

ALEXANDER VON HUMBOLDT

Alexander von Humboldt (1769–1859) was a Prussian scientist from Berlin who helped map and study North America in a truly scientific way. In 1799, he and French botanist Aimé Bonpland set sail from Marseille for the New World on a voyage of scientific discovery.

Humboldt was an energetic and tough explorer, traveling through dense forest, climbing high mountain peaks, canoeing up tropical rivers though clouds of mosquitoes and surviving on a minimal diet. He recorded everything from the plants he came across to the heights of the mountains, as well as animals, minerals, and ancient artifacts.

At a time when most accounts of the new world were still filled with exaggeration and mystery, he made sure to measure and record everything he saw with total accuracy, using the very latest equipment. His expeditions covered a total of nearly 6,200 miles. Humboldt's interests drew together an extraordinary range of studies, from geology and minerals to magnetism, botany, zoology, astronomy, weather and climate, ocean currents, history, economics, and society. He understood the networks and processes that support life on Earth and even then was concerned about the impact of humans on the environment and on climate.

As a scientist, Humboldt took detailed measurements and looked for new ways of showing data that everyone could understand, such as isobars (lines drawn on a map to show equal pressure points within a weather system). He even used his measurements to describe man-made climate change for the first time ever.

1617	1799	1800-1804	1826-1830	1832-35	1848-52
Walter Raleigh returns to Guiana, for a second mission, but still finds no trace of El Dorado.	Geographer and scientist Alexander von Humboldt explores Venezuela.	Humboldt explores Cuba, the Andes Mountains and Mexico.	British hydrographic survey of Tierra del Fuego by HMS *Beagle*.	Charles Darwin, naturalist on HMS *Beagle*, explores the South American coast.	Alfred Russel Wallace explores the Amazon basin, its plants, animals, peoples and languages.

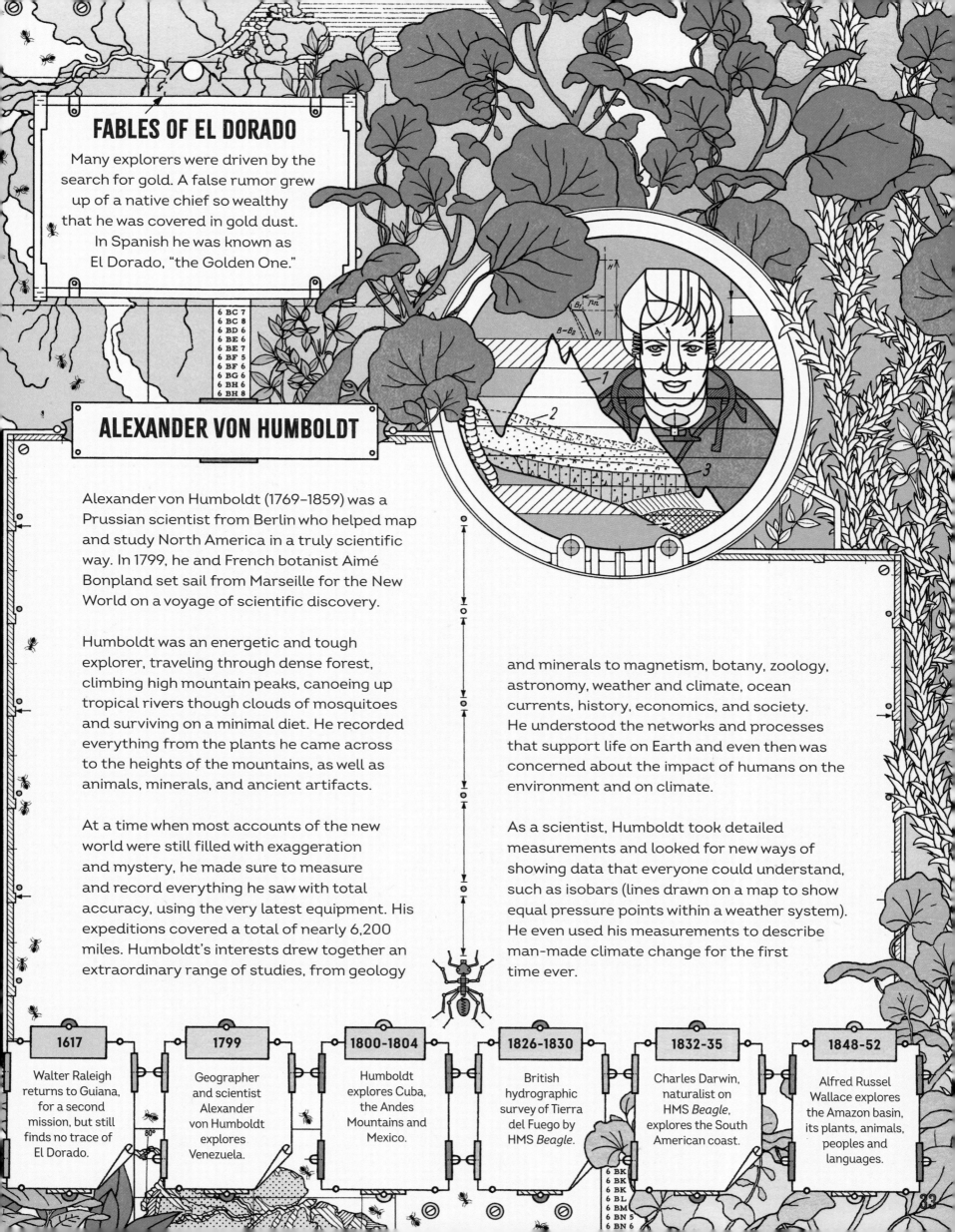

ROBERT BURKE AND WILLIAM WILLS

In 1860 Robert Burke and William Wills set out for the northern coast of Australia from Melbourne. They crossed harsh deserts and reached the northern shore, but the journey was fraught with danger.

ACROSS OCEANIA

Australia 300 years ago was a land of red rocks and sweltering deserts, ringed by rolling surf. To the east were the snowy peaks of New Zealand and the Pacific Ocean. European explorers sailed here in search of "unknown" lands. But the Aborigines and Pacific islanders had already known the secrets of Oceania for thousands of years . . .

VIEW THIS PAGE IN THE APP
TO SEE THE JOURNEYS

ROBERT BURKE AND WILLIAM WILLS
Melbourne, 1860

ABEL TASMAN
Southern Ocean, 1642

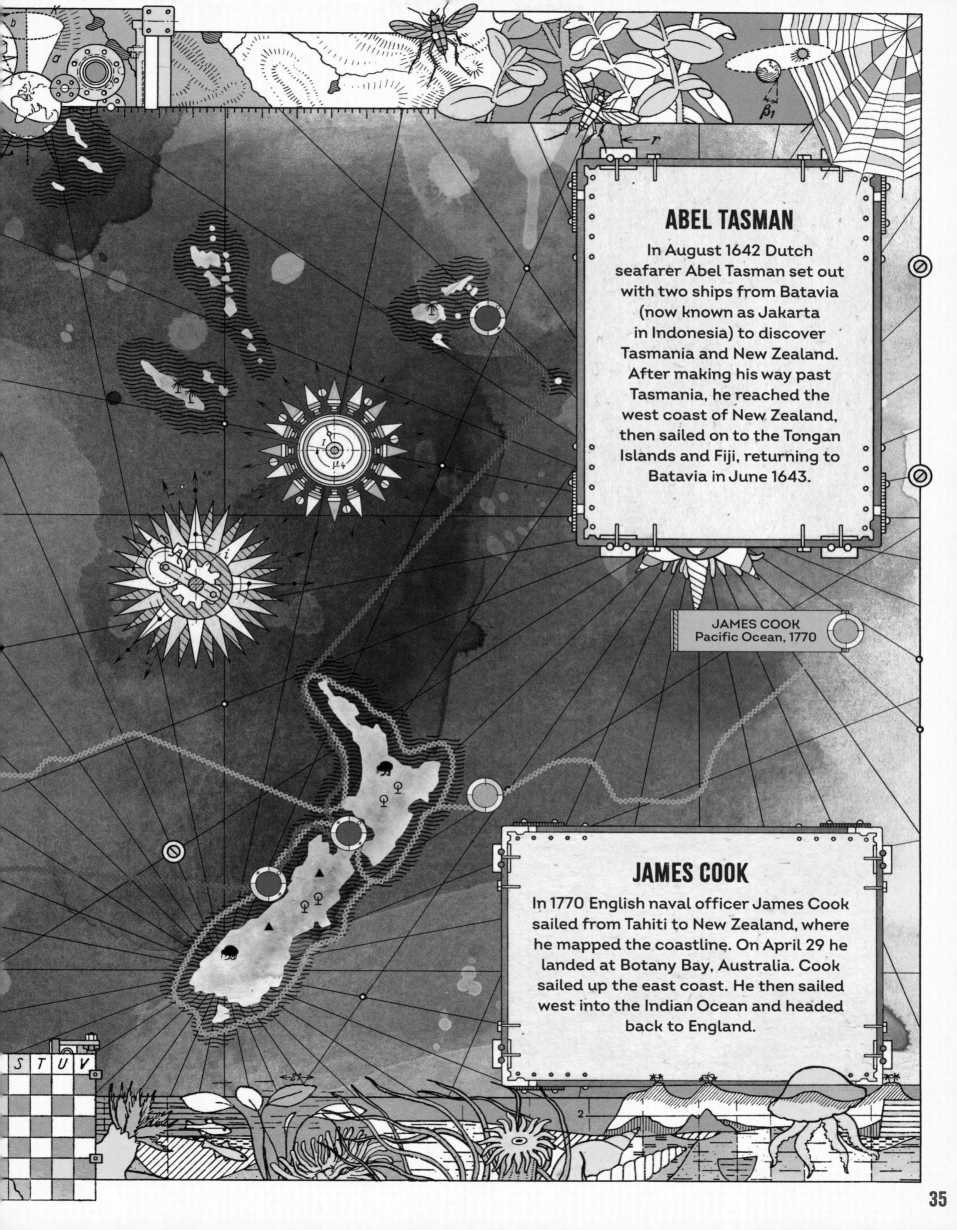

ABEL TASMAN

In August 1642 Dutch seafarer Abel Tasman set out with two ships from Batavia (now known as Jakarta in Indonesia) to discover Tasmania and New Zealand. After making his way past Tasmania, he reached the west coast of New Zealand, then sailed on to the Tongan Islands and Fiji, returning to Batavia in June 1643.

JAMES COOK
Pacific Ocean, 1770

JAMES COOK

In 1770 English naval officer James Cook sailed from Tahiti to New Zealand, where he mapped the coastline. On April 29 he landed at Botany Bay, Australia. Cook sailed up the east coast. He then sailed west into the Indian Ocean and headed back to England.

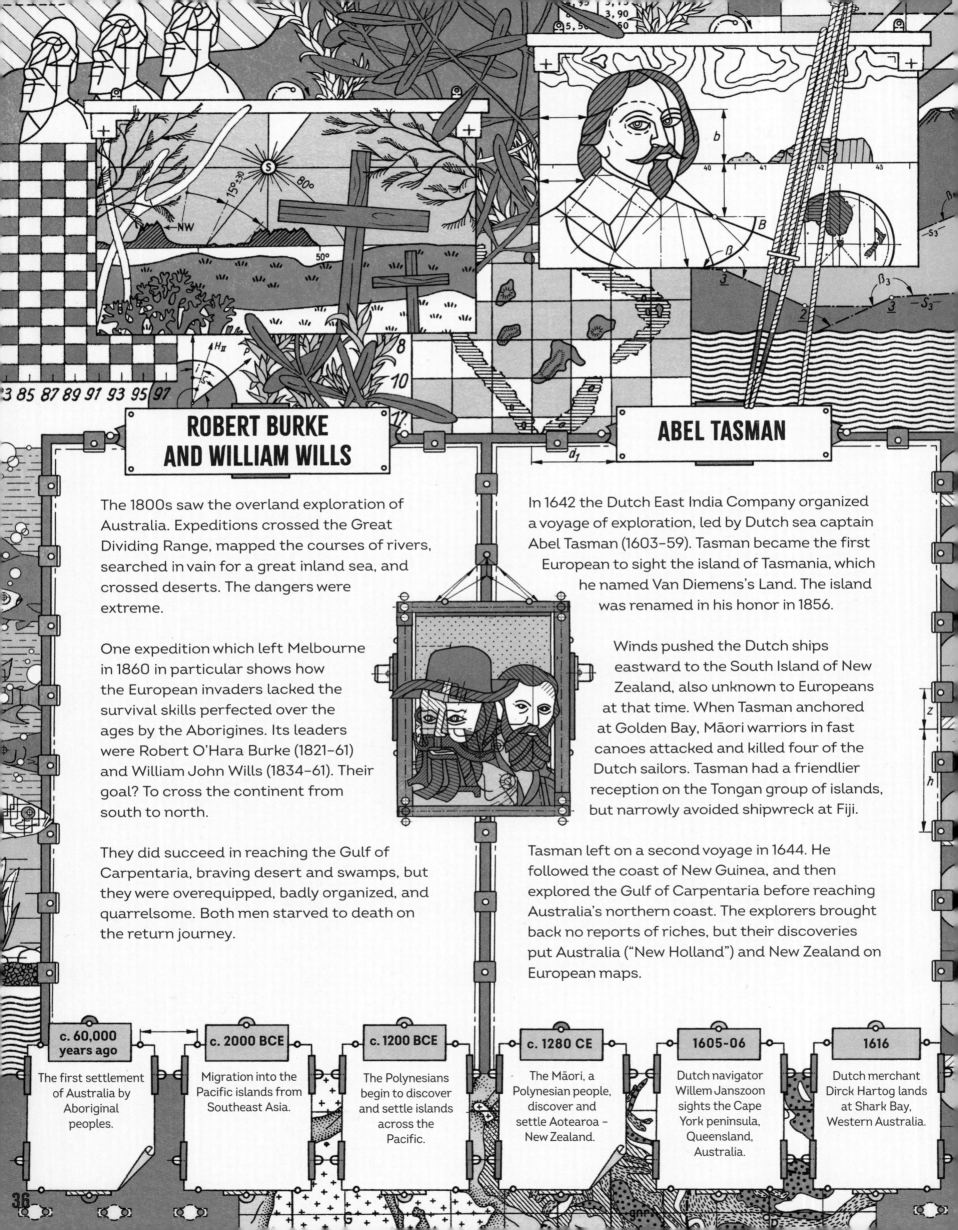

ROBERT BURKE AND WILLIAM WILLS

The 1800s saw the overland exploration of Australia. Expeditions crossed the Great Dividing Range, mapped the courses of rivers, searched in vain for a great inland sea, and crossed deserts. The dangers were extreme.

One expedition which left Melbourne in 1860 in particular shows how the European invaders lacked the survival skills perfected over the ages by the Aborigines. Its leaders were Robert O'Hara Burke (1821–61) and William John Wills (1834–61). Their goal? To cross the continent from south to north.

They did succeed in reaching the Gulf of Carpentaria, braving desert and swamps, but they were overequipped, badly organized, and quarrelsome. Both men starved to death on the return journey.

ABEL TASMAN

In 1642 the Dutch East India Company organized a voyage of exploration, led by Dutch sea captain Abel Tasman (1603–59). Tasman became the first European to sight the island of Tasmania, which he named Van Diemens's Land. The island was renamed in his honor in 1856.

Winds pushed the Dutch ships eastward to the South Island of New Zealand, also unknown to Europeans at that time. When Tasman anchored at Golden Bay, Māori warriors in fast canoes attacked and killed four of the Dutch sailors. Tasman had a friendlier reception on the Tongan group of islands, but narrowly avoided shipwreck at Fiji.

Tasman left on a second voyage in 1644. He followed the coast of New Guinea, and then explored the Gulf of Carpentaria before reaching Australia's northern coast. The explorers brought back no reports of riches, but their discoveries put Australia ("New Holland") and New Zealand on European maps.

c. 60,000 years ago	c. 2000 BCE	c. 1200 BCE	c. 1280 CE	1605–06	1616
The first settlement of Australia by Aboriginal peoples.	Migration into the Pacific islands from Southeast Asia.	The Polynesians begin to discover and settle islands across the Pacific.	The Māori, a Polynesian people, discover and settle Aotearoa – New Zealand.	Dutch navigator Willem Janszoon sights the Cape York peninsula, Queensland, Australia.	Dutch merchant Dirck Hartog lands at Shark Bay, Western Australia.

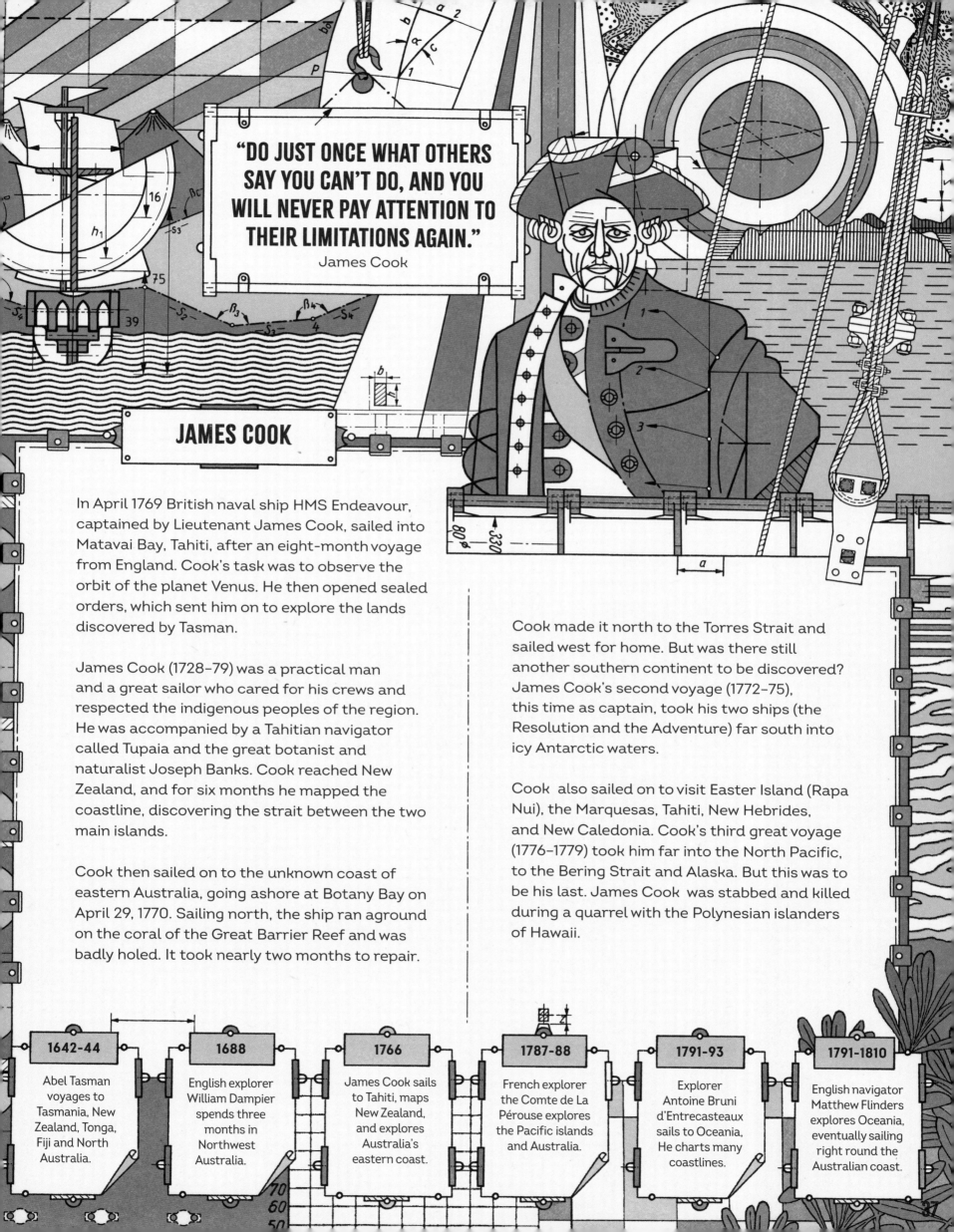

> **"DO JUST ONCE WHAT OTHERS SAY YOU CAN'T DO, AND YOU WILL NEVER PAY ATTENTION TO THEIR LIMITATIONS AGAIN."**
> James Cook

JAMES COOK

In April 1769 British naval ship HMS Endeavour, captained by Lieutenant James Cook, sailed into Matavai Bay, Tahiti, after an eight-month voyage from England. Cook's task was to observe the orbit of the planet Venus. He then opened sealed orders, which sent him on to explore the lands discovered by Tasman.

James Cook (1728–79) was a practical man and a great sailor who cared for his crews and respected the indigenous peoples of the region. He was accompanied by a Tahitian navigator called Tupaia and the great botanist and naturalist Joseph Banks. Cook reached New Zealand, and for six months he mapped the coastline, discovering the strait between the two main islands.

Cook then sailed on to the unknown coast of eastern Australia, going ashore at Botany Bay on April 29, 1770. Sailing north, the ship ran aground on the coral of the Great Barrier Reef and was badly holed. It took nearly two months to repair.

Cook made it north to the Torres Strait and sailed west for home. But was there still another southern continent to be discovered? James Cook's second voyage (1772–75), this time as captain, took his two ships (the Resolution and the Adventure) far south into icy Antarctic waters.

Cook also sailed on to visit Easter Island (Rapa Nui), the Marquesas, Tahiti, New Hebrides, and New Caledonia. Cook's third great voyage (1776–1779) took him far into the North Pacific, to the Bering Strait and Alaska. But this was to be his last. James Cook was stabbed and killed during a quarrel with the Polynesian islanders of Hawaii.

Timeline

1642-44
Abel Tasman voyages to Tasmania, New Zealand, Tonga, Fiji and North Australia.

1688
English explorer William Dampier spends three months in Northwest Australia.

1766
James Cook sails to Tahiti, maps New Zealand, and explores Australia's eastern coast.

1787-88
French explorer the Comte de La Pérouse explores the Pacific islands and Australia.

1791-93
Explorer Antoine Bruni d'Entrecasteaux sails to Oceania, He charts many coastlines.

1791-1810
English navigator Matthew Flinders explores Oceania, eventually sailing right round the Australian coast.

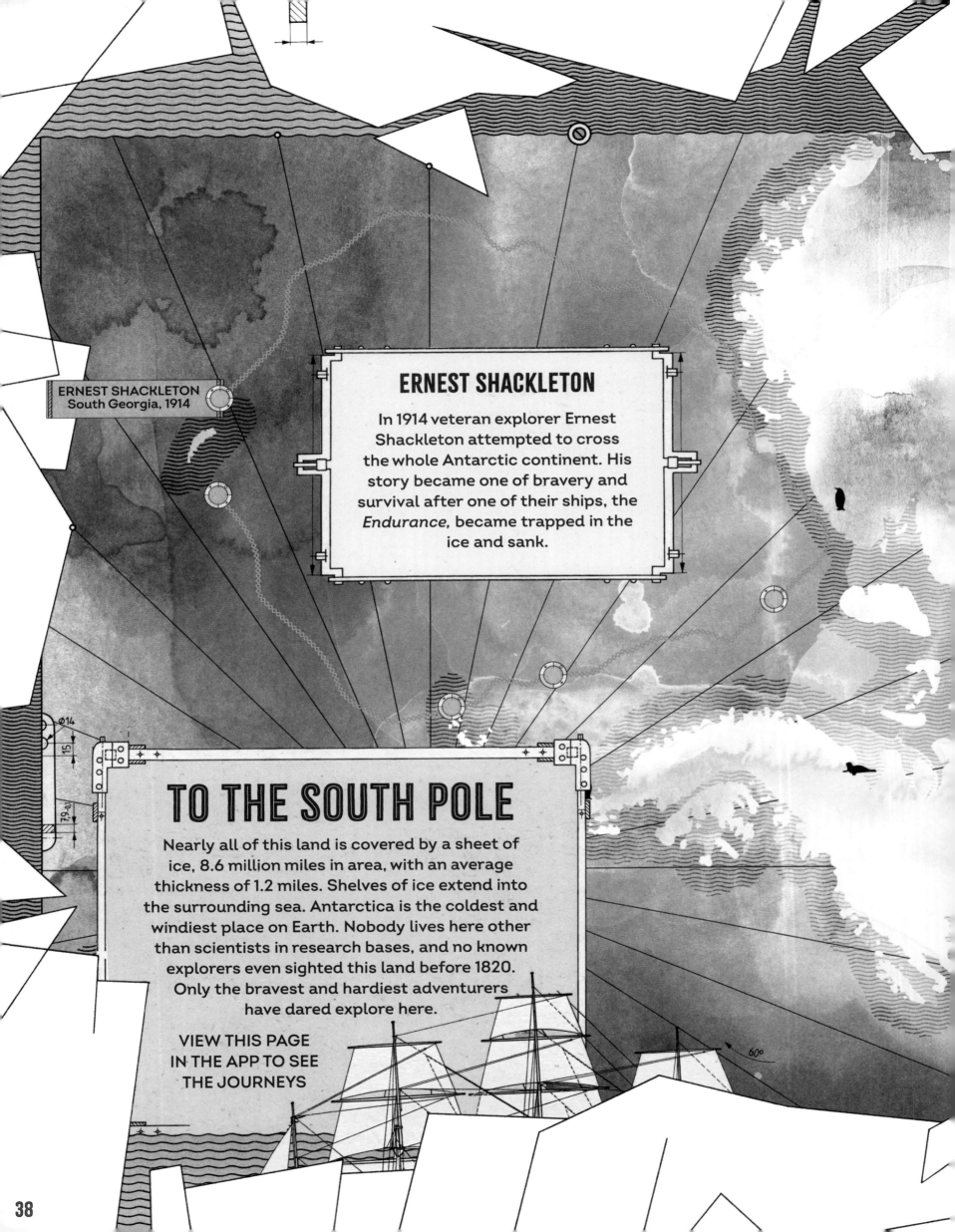

ERNEST SHACKLETON
South Georgia, 1914

ERNEST SHACKLETON

In 1914 veteran explorer Ernest Shackleton attempted to cross the whole Antarctic continent. His story became one of bravery and survival after one of their ships, the *Endurance,* became trapped in the ice and sank.

TO THE SOUTH POLE

Nearly all of this land is covered by a sheet of ice, 8.6 million miles in area, with an average thickness of 1.2 miles. Shelves of ice extend into the surrounding sea. Antarctica is the coldest and windiest place on Earth. Nobody lives here other than scientists in research bases, and no known explorers even sighted this land before 1820. Only the bravest and hardiest adventurers have dared explore here.

VIEW THIS PAGE IN THE APP TO SEE THE JOURNEYS

ROBERT FALCON SCOTT

On Scott's second Antarctic expedition, the team reached the Pole on January 17, 1912, only to find that Amundsen had gotten there first. Their 186-mile return journey was a disaster, and all four team members died just 11 miles from safety.

ROBERT FALCON SCOTT
Ross Island, 1912

ROALD AMUNDSEN
Bay of Whales, 1911

ROALD AMUNDSEN

In 1911 and 1912, Norwegian explorer Roald Amundsen's team became the first to reach the South Pole. They made their way to the Pole in 56 days using skis, and sleds hauled by teams of dogs.

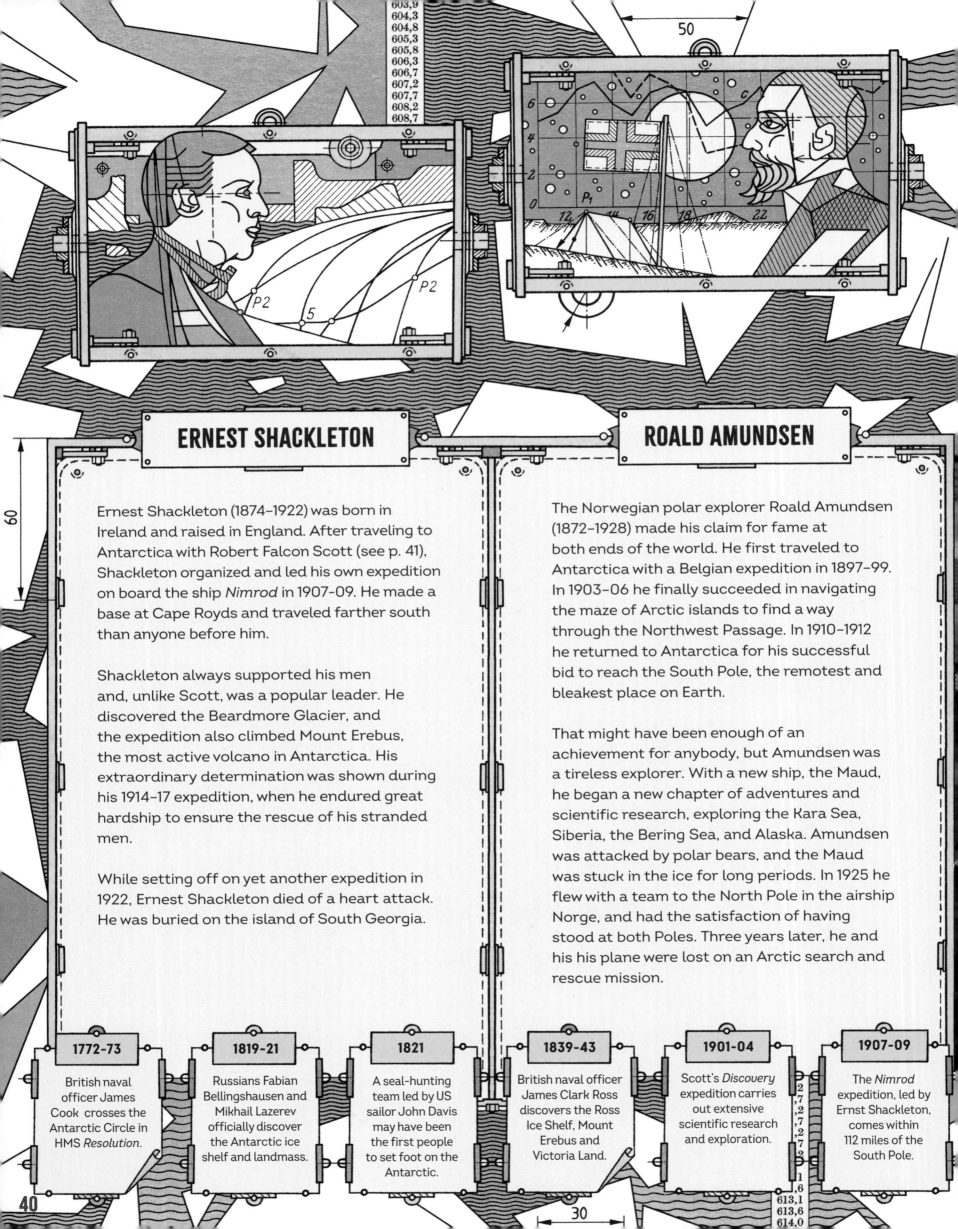

ERNEST SHACKLETON

Ernest Shackleton (1874–1922) was born in Ireland and raised in England. After traveling to Antarctica with Robert Falcon Scott (see p. 41), Shackleton organized and led his own expedition on board the ship *Nimrod* in 1907–09. He made a base at Cape Royds and traveled farther south than anyone before him.

Shackleton always supported his men and, unlike Scott, was a popular leader. He discovered the Beardmore Glacier, and the expedition also climbed Mount Erebus, the most active volcano in Antarctica. His extraordinary determination was shown during his 1914–17 expedition, when he endured great hardship to ensure the rescue of his stranded men.

While setting off on yet another expedition in 1922, Ernest Shackleton died of a heart attack. He was buried on the island of South Georgia.

ROALD AMUNDSEN

The Norwegian polar explorer Roald Amundsen (1872–1928) made his claim for fame at both ends of the world. He first traveled to Antarctica with a Belgian expedition in 1897–99. In 1903–06 he finally succeeded in navigating the maze of Arctic islands to find a way through the Northwest Passage. In 1910–1912 he returned to Antarctica for his successful bid to reach the South Pole, the remotest and bleakest place on Earth.

That might have been enough of an achievement for anybody, but Amundsen was a tireless explorer. With a new ship, the Maud, he began a new chapter of adventures and scientific research, exploring the Kara Sea, Siberia, the Bering Sea, and Alaska. Amundsen was attacked by polar bears, and the Maud was stuck in the ice for long periods. In 1925 he flew with a team to the North Pole in the airship Norge, and had the satisfaction of having stood at both Poles. Three years later, he and his his plane were lost on an Arctic search and rescue mission.

1772–73
British naval officer James Cook crosses the Antarctic Circle in HMS *Resolution*.

1819–21
Russians Fabian Bellingshausen and Mikhail Lazerev officially discover the Antarctic ice shelf and landmass.

1821
A seal-hunting team led by US sailor John Davis may have been the first people to set foot on the Antarctic.

1839–43
British naval officer James Clark Ross discovers the Ross Ice Shelf, Mount Erebus and Victoria Land.

1901–04
Scott's *Discovery* expedition carries out extensive scientific research and exploration.

1907–09
The *Nimrod* expedition, led by Ernst Shackleton, comes within 112 miles of the South Pole.

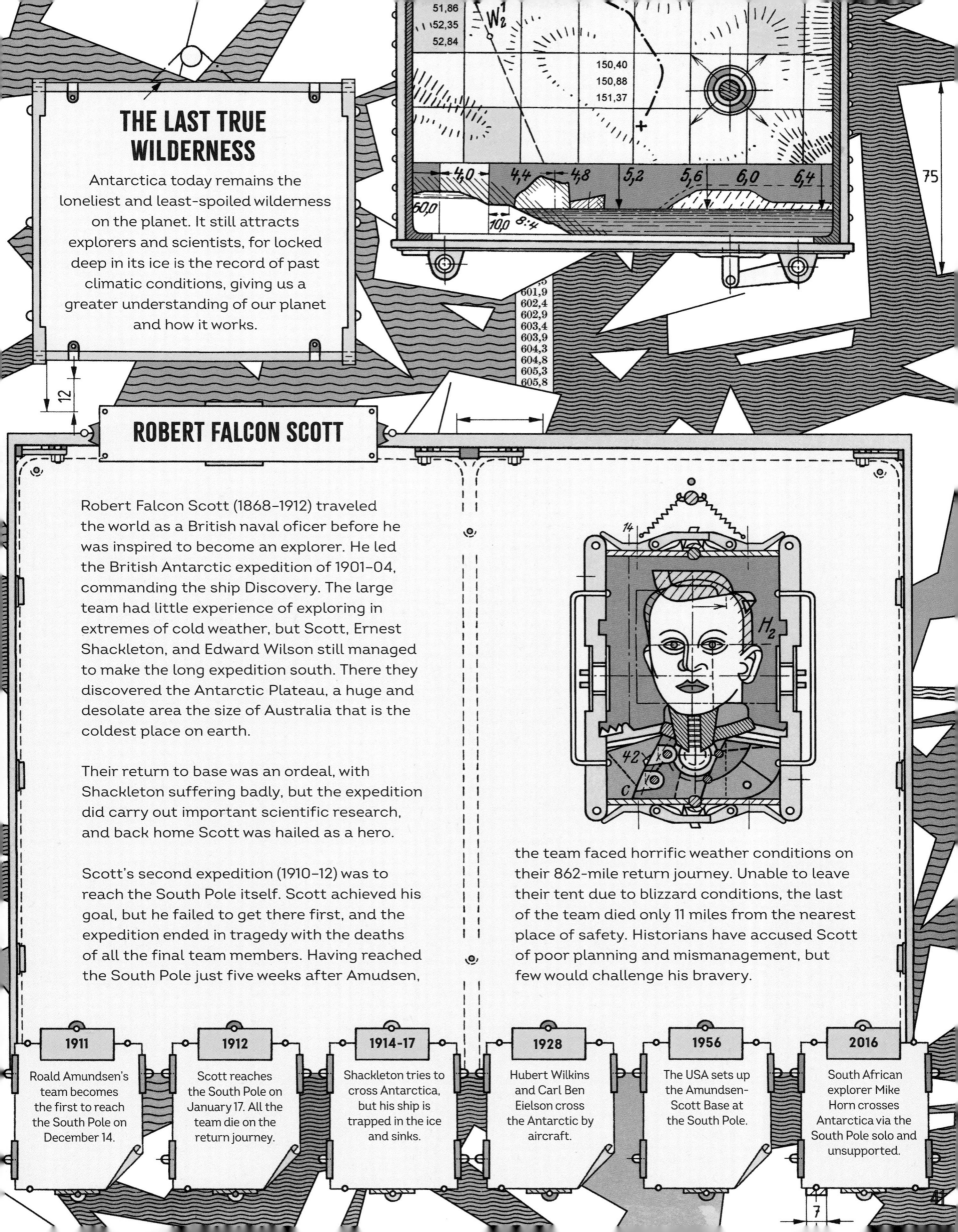

THE LAST TRUE WILDERNESS

Antarctica today remains the loneliest and least-spoiled wilderness on the planet. It still attracts explorers and scientists, for locked deep in its ice is the record of past climatic conditions, giving us a greater understanding of our planet and how it works.

ROBERT FALCON SCOTT

Robert Falcon Scott (1868–1912) traveled the world as a British naval oficer before he was inspired to become an explorer. He led the British Antarctic expedition of 1901–04, commanding the ship Discovery. The large team had little experience of exploring in extremes of cold weather, but Scott, Ernest Shackleton, and Edward Wilson still managed to make the long expedition south. There they discovered the Antarctic Plateau, a huge and desolate area the size of Australia that is the coldest place on earth.

Their return to base was an ordeal, with Shackleton suffering badly, but the expedition did carry out important scientific research, and back home Scott was hailed as a hero.

Scott's second expedition (1910–12) was to reach the South Pole itself. Scott achieved his goal, but he failed to get there first, and the expedition ended in tragedy with the deaths of all the final team members. Having reached the South Pole just five weeks after Amudsen,

the team faced horrific weather conditions on their 862-mile return journey. Unable to leave their tent due to blizzard conditions, the last of the team died only 11 miles from the nearest place of safety. Historians have accused Scott of poor planning and mismanagement, but few would challenge his bravery.

1911	**1912**	**1914–17**	**1928**	**1956**	**2016**
Roald Amundsen's team becomes the first to reach the South Pole on December 14.	Scott reaches the South Pole on January 17. All the team die on the return journey.	Shackleton tries to cross Antarctica, but his ship is trapped in the ice and sinks.	Hubert Wilkins and Carl Ben Eielson cross the Antarctic by aircraft.	The USA sets up the Amundsen-Scott Base at the South Pole.	South African explorer Mike Horn crosses Antarctica via the South Pole solo and unsupported.

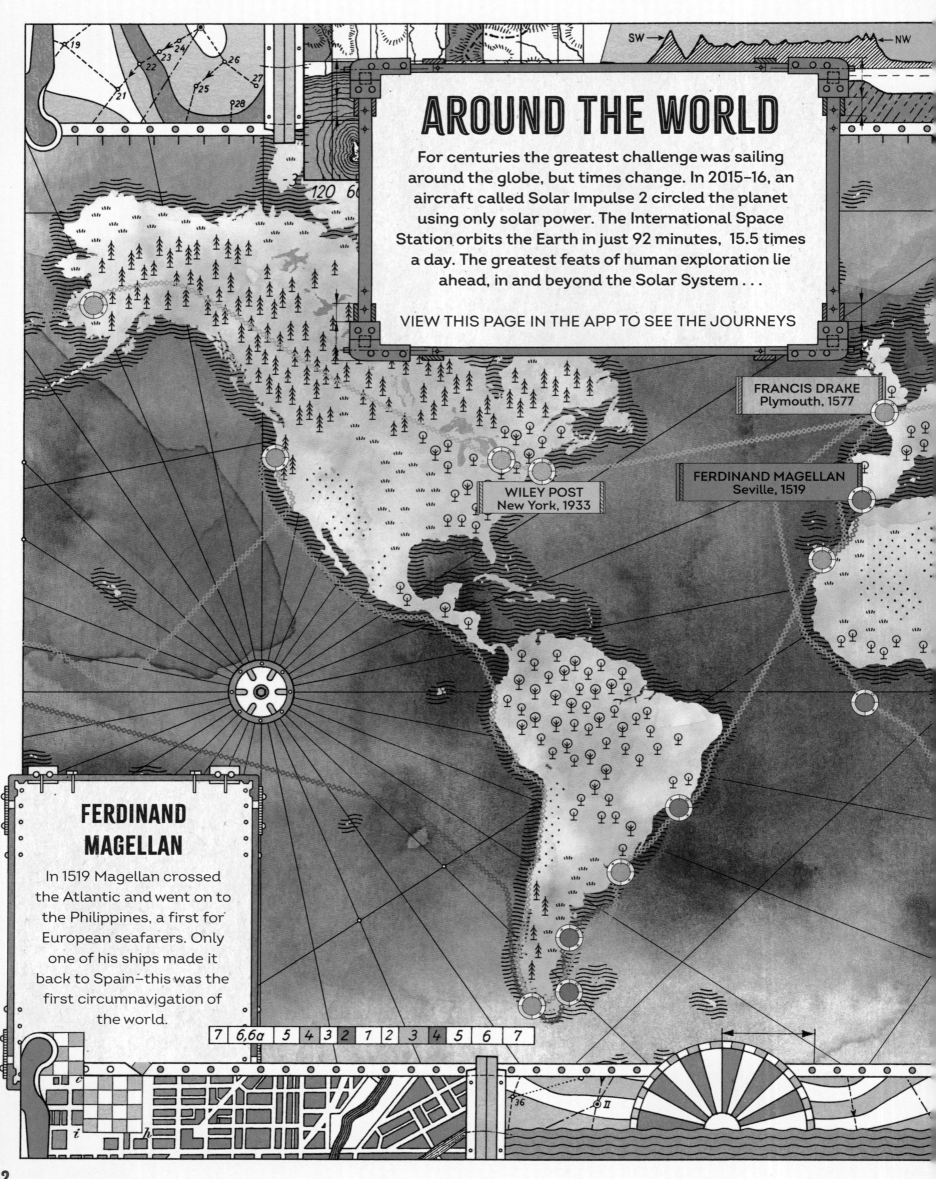

AROUND THE WORLD

For centuries the greatest challenge was sailing around the globe, but times change. In 2015–16, an aircraft called Solar Impulse 2 circled the planet using only solar power. The International Space Station orbits the Earth in just 92 minutes, 15.5 times a day. The greatest feats of human exploration lie ahead, in and beyond the Solar System . . .

VIEW THIS PAGE IN THE APP TO SEE THE JOURNEYS

FRANCIS DRAKE
Plymouth, 1577

WILEY POST
New York, 1933

FERDINAND MAGELLAN
Seville, 1519

FERDINAND MAGELLAN

In 1519 Magellan crossed the Atlantic and went on to the Philippines, a first for European seafarers. Only one of his ships made it back to Spain–this was the first circumnavigation of the world.

SW →   ← NW

WILEY POST

A group of US Army biplanes were the first to circumnavigate the globe in 1924. But the first pilot to navigate the world solo was US aviator Wiley Post in 1933. He took just 7 days, 18 hours, 49 minutes. The world had shrunk!

FRANCIS DRAKE

In 1577 Queen Elizabeth I of England sent Francis Drake to raid Spanish colonists around the Pacific. He sailed there through the Strait of Magellan in 1578. Drake looted Spanish ships and attacked settlements. He landed in California and "claimed" it for England. He arrived back in Plymouth in 1580.

0,0153
0,0163
0,0174
0,0186
0,0197
0,0211
0,0224
0,0238

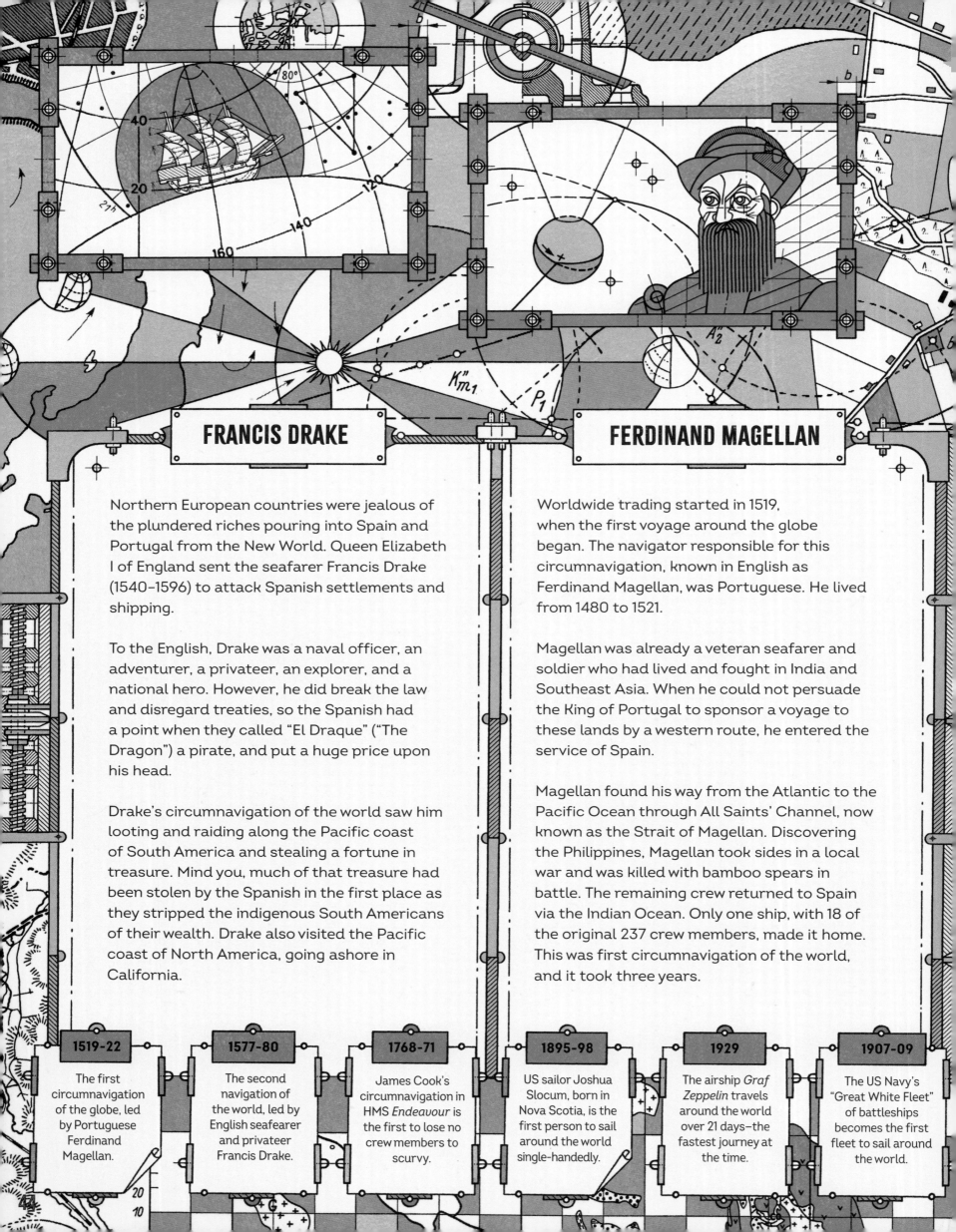

FRANCIS DRAKE

Northern European countries were jealous of the plundered riches pouring into Spain and Portugal from the New World. Queen Elizabeth I of England sent the seafarer Francis Drake (1540–1596) to attack Spanish settlements and shipping.

To the English, Drake was a naval officer, an adventurer, a privateer, an explorer, and a national hero. However, he did break the law and disregard treaties, so the Spanish had a point when they called "El Draque" ("The Dragon") a pirate, and put a huge price upon his head.

Drake's circumnavigation of the world saw him looting and raiding along the Pacific coast of South America and stealing a fortune in treasure. Mind you, much of that treasure had been stolen by the Spanish in the first place as they stripped the indigenous South Americans of their wealth. Drake also visited the Pacific coast of North America, going ashore in California.

FERDINAND MAGELLAN

Worldwide trading started in 1519, when the first voyage around the globe began. The navigator responsible for this circumnavigation, known in English as Ferdinand Magellan, was Portuguese. He lived from 1480 to 1521.

Magellan was already a veteran seafarer and soldier who had lived and fought in India and Southeast Asia. When he could not persuade the King of Portugal to sponsor a voyage to these lands by a western route, he entered the service of Spain.

Magellan found his way from the Atlantic to the Pacific Ocean through All Saints' Channel, now known as the Strait of Magellan. Discovering the Philippines, Magellan took sides in a local war and was killed with bamboo spears in battle. The remaining crew returned to Spain via the Indian Ocean. Only one ship, with 18 of the original 237 crew members, made it home. This was first circumnavigation of the world, and it took three years.

1519–22
The first circumnavigation of the globe, led by Portuguese Ferdinand Magellan.

1577–80
The second navigation of the world, led by English seafarer and privateer Francis Drake.

1768–71
James Cook's circumnavigation in HMS *Endeavour* is the first to lose no crew members to scurvy.

1895–98
US sailor Joshua Slocum, born in Nova Scotia, is the first person to sail around the world single-handedly.

1929
The airship *Graf Zeppelin* travels around the world over 21 days–the fastest journey at the time.

1907–09
The US Navy's "Great White Fleet" of battleships becomes the first fleet to sail around the world.

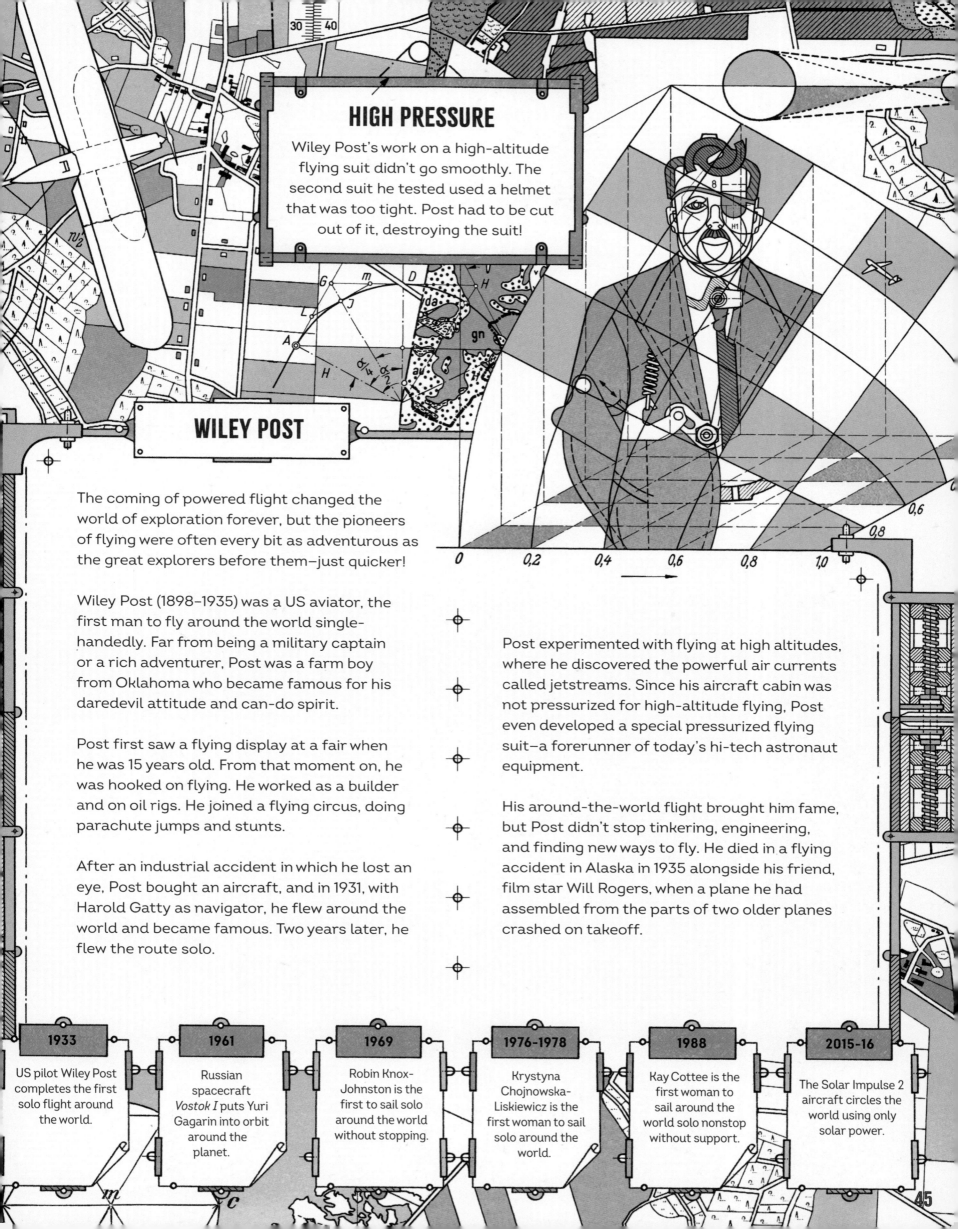

HIGH PRESSURE

Wiley Post's work on a high-altitude flying suit didn't go smoothly. The second suit he tested used a helmet that was too tight. Post had to be cut out of it, destroying the suit!

WILEY POST

The coming of powered flight changed the world of exploration forever, but the pioneers of flying were often every bit as adventurous as the great explorers before them—just quicker!

Wiley Post (1898–1935) was a US aviator, the first man to fly around the world single-handedly. Far from being a military captain or a rich adventurer, Post was a farm boy from Oklahoma who became famous for his daredevil attitude and can-do spirit.

Post first saw a flying display at a fair when he was 15 years old. From that moment on, he was hooked on flying. He worked as a builder and on oil rigs. He joined a flying circus, doing parachute jumps and stunts.

After an industrial accident in which he lost an eye, Post bought an aircraft, and in 1931, with Harold Gatty as navigator, he flew around the world and became famous. Two years later, he flew the route solo.

Post experimented with flying at high altitudes, where he discovered the powerful air currents called jetstreams. Since his aircraft cabin was not pressurized for high-altitude flying, Post even developed a special pressurized flying suit—a forerunner of today's hi-tech astronaut equipment.

His around-the-world flight brought him fame, but Post didn't stop tinkering, engineering, and finding new ways to fly. He died in a flying accident in Alaska in 1935 alongside his friend, film star Will Rogers, when a plane he had assembled from the parts of two older planes crashed on takeoff.

1933
US pilot Wiley Post completes the first solo flight around the world.

1961
Russian spacecraft *Vostok I* puts Yuri Gagarin into orbit around the planet.

1969
Robin Knox-Johnston is the first to sail solo around the world without stopping.

1976–1978
Krystyna Chojnowska-Liskiewicz is the first woman to sail solo around the world.

1988
Kay Cottee is the first woman to sail around the world solo nonstop without support.

2015-16
The Solar Impulse 2 aircraft circles the world using only solar power.

GLOSSARY

ABORIGINE 1 A member of Australia's oldest ethnic group. 2 A member of an ethnic group which has lived in a country from earliest times.

ACADEMIC Concerned with scholarship and study at an advanced level.

AGE OF DISCOVERY A name sometimes given to the period between the 1400s and the 1600s, when Europeans explored the world and its oceans.

AIRSHIP A powered aircraft that is lifted by gas which is lighter than air. Airships were in wide use from the 1900s to the 1930s.

ANCHORAGE An offshore location where depth and shelter are suitable for a ship to drop anchor.

ANTARCTIC The land, ice shelves, islands and ocean around the South Pole, below the latitude of 66.5°S.

ARCTIC The ocean, ice sheets, lands and islands around the North Pole, above the latitude of 66.5°N.

AVIATOR The pilot of an airplane, a term often used to describe the pioneers of flying and aerial exploration.

BIPLANE A twin-winged aircraft. A triplane has three wings, a monoplane one wing.

BOTANY The scientific study of plants. A plant scientist is a botanist.

CIRCUMNAVIGATE To travel all the way around something, such as an island or the whole world.

CONQUISTADORS Soldiers and armed explorers who conquered, looted and colonized large areas of the Americas (the "New World") from the 1500s.

CONTINENT A large section of continuous land. They are named by geographers as Europe, Asia, Africa, Australia, North America, South America, and Antarctica.

CURRENT A strong directional movement of water in an ocean, sea or river.

DIPLOMACY The negotiating of agreements, relationships and alliances between nations and other groups of people.

ELDORADO El Dorado or Eldorado meant "the Golden One", and referred to a legendary ruler said to live in South America. The term came to mean a rumored land of fabulous wealth, sought after in vain by European explorers of the 1500s and 1600s.

EMPIRE A large group of countries and territories ruled over by a single monarch, called an emperor, or by a single nation.

EQUATOR An imaginary line drawn around the middle of the planet at the latitude of 0°, at equal distance from both Poles.

EXPEDITION A journey organised for a particular purpose, such as exploration or mountain climbing.

GANGRENE A serious medical condition created by loss of blood supply to part of the body.

GENOCIDE The deliberate killing of very large groups of people, especially because of their nationality or ethnicity.

GEOGRAPHY The study of the Earth, its climate, natural history, landscapes, populations and nations. A geography expert is called a geographer.

GEOLOGY The study of the Earth, its rocks and their formation. A rock scientist is called a geologist.

HOMO SAPIENS The scientific name for the only living human species.

INDIGENOUS Native to a country, belonging to the local ethnic group or groups.

LAND BRIDGE A connecting strip between two landmasses at a time of low sea levels.

LANDMASS A large connected area of land. Europe and Asia are part of the same landmass.

MALARIA A dangerous illness which is passed on to humans by certain mosquito parasites.

METEOROLOGY The study of weather conditions and the Earth's atmosphere. A weather scientist is called a meteorologist.

MIGRATE Of people, animals or birds, to move from one place to another.

MONOPLANE A single-winged airplane.

NAVIGATOR 1 A marine explorer. 2 The person who is responsible for plotting the course of a ship or airplane.

OCEAN One of the huge bodies of salty water which cover about 71 percent of the Earth's surface.

ORE A metal-bearing rock. The metal can be separated by being heated in a furnace, a process called smelting.

PHARAOH A word we use today to describe a ruler of Ancient Egypt.

PILGRIMAGE A long journey carried out for religious reasons, such as visiting a holy site.

PIRATE A robber of ships at sea or a coastal raider.

POLES The extreme ends of the axis which the Earth spins around, the northern and southernmost points on the planet.

RAINFOREST An ancient and very rich ecosystem of dense forest and high rainfall, either tropical or temperate.

REFUGEE Somebody who flees to another country in order to escape war, persecution, famine, poverty or a natural disaster.

SILK ROAD A network of trading routes linking China with western Asia and southern Europe from about 200 BCE until the 1600s.

SOURCE The origin of a great river, such as the Nile or the Amazon.

STRAIT A narrow strip of water linking two larger bodies of water.

SURVEYOR Somebody who measures or charts land or coastlines.

TERRAIN The landscape of a location, its height, steepness and vegetation.

TERRITORY An area of land, generally one which comes under the rule of another state.

TREATY A formal agreement between two or more countries.

TRIBUTES Taxes, gifts or or goods sent to an emperor from the lands he rules.

ZOOLOGY The study of animal life. An animal scientist is called a zoologist.

INDEX